HOW TO DRAW WINGS and WHEELS

kidsbooks ®
Incorporated

Copyright © 1994 Kidsbooks Inc.
3535 West Peterson Avenue
Chicago, IL 60659

Manufactured in the United States of America

Visit us at www.kidsbooks.com
Volume discounts available for group purchases.

Introduction

This book will show you some easy ways to draw lots of different cars, trucks, and aircraft. Some may be more difficult than others, but if you follow along, step-by-step, you'll soon be able to draw many different things with wheels and wings.

Using the basic shapes illustrated below will help you get started. Remember that these shapes, in different sizes and combinations, will change from drawing to drawing. Variations of these shapes will also be used. Refer, too, to the terms listed. They will help you refine and complete your pictures.

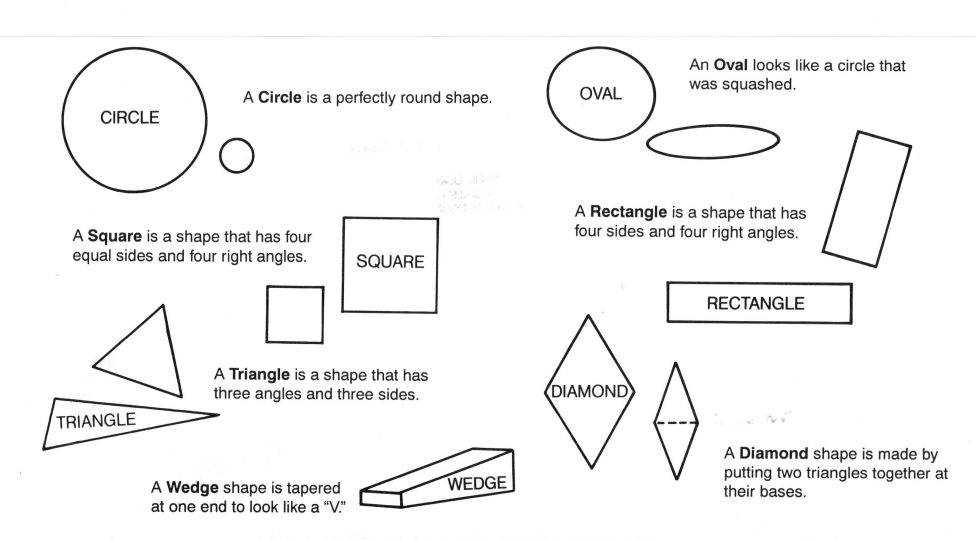

CIRCLE

A **Circle** is a perfectly round shape.

OVAL

An **Oval** looks like a circle that was squashed.

A **Square** is a shape that has four equal sides and four right angles.

SQUARE

A **Rectangle** is a shape that has four sides and four right angles.

RECTANGLE

A **Triangle** is a shape that has three angles and three sides.

TRIANGLE

DIAMOND

A **Diamond** shape is made by putting two triangles together at their bases.

A **Wedge** shape is tapered at one end to look like a "V."

WEDGE

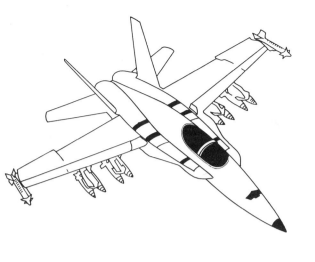

Supplies

NUMBER 2 PENCILS
SOFT ERASER
DRAWING PAD
FELT-TIP PEN (thick and thin points)
COLORED PENCILS, MARKERS
OR CRAYONS

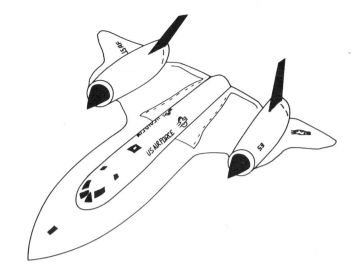

IMPORTANT TERMS:

BUTT Joining objects end to end, but not overlapping them.

OVERLAP To cover one part of an object with part of another object.

DIMENSION Objects have three dimensions: width, height, and depth.

PERSPECTIVE When you show an object's three dimensions, you are showing it in perspective and from a viewpoint.

VIEWPOINT is the position from which you see an object. Examples: top view, side view, rear view; or a combination like front side view.

CONTOUR The shape of an object or its outline.

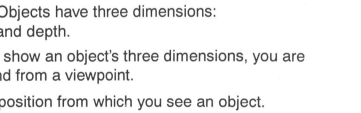

HELPFUL HINTS

Following these steps carefully will help you master the art of drawing.

1. **Always keep your initial pencil lines light and soft.**
   These "guidelines" will be easier to erase when you no longer need them.

2. **Don't be afraid to erase.**
   It usually takes lots of drawing and erasing before you will be satisfied with the way your picture looks.

3. Add details and the finishing touches **after** you have blended and refined the lines and shapes and completed the basic drawing.

4. Remember: **Practice Makes Perfect**
   Don't get discouraged if you can't get the "hang of it" right away. Just keep drawing and erasing until you do.

HOW TO START

Before starting your first drawing, you may want to practice tracing the different steps.

Start your drawing by lightly sketching out the first step. The first step is very important and should be done carefully. The second step will be sketched over the first one. Next, refine and blend the shapes together, erasing any guidelines you no longer need. Add final details. When your drawing is complete, go over your pencil lines with a felt-tip pen. You might want to draw a thicker line for the outer shape of your vehicle or aircraft and a thinner line for the contours and details. If you wish, you may color your drawing with markers, pencils, or crayons.

Each car, truck, or aircraft has special characteristics that make it easier or, in some cases, more difficult to draw. However, it's easy to draw anything when you break it down into simple shapes! Remember, practice makes perfect, so keep sketching and erasing until you've mastered each drawing. Use your imagination. Add drivers, roads, pilots, clouds, and backgrounds; create a scene with two or more vehicles, or several aircraft, or both! Most of all, HAVE FUN!

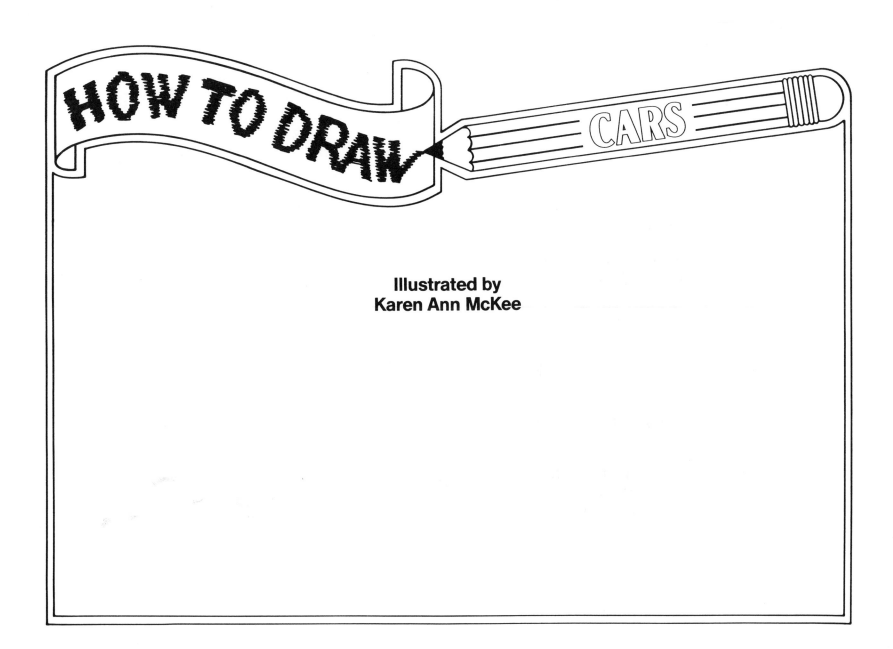

HOW TO DRAW CARS

Illustrated by
Karen Ann McKee

1985 Lamborghini Countach

This hot car has been making gut-wrenching getaways since its introduction in 1971. The Countach zooms from 0-60 in 5.9 seconds. Collectible models sell easily for $100,000 to upwards of $200,000!

1. Start with a large 4-sided shape to form the hood and one side of the car. Add a rectangular shape for the front bumper, and finish the side panel with lines that form a wedge, as shown. Then draw two oval guidelines for each visible tire.

Note: It is always easier to draw the largest shape first, then add the smaller shapes.

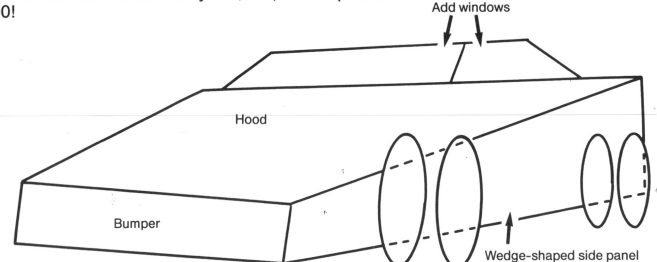

Add windows

Hood

Bumper

Wedge-shaped side panel

2. Next, add three curved lines to shape the hood of the car. Then connect each pair of ovals to form the tires. Draw a line to divide the front bumper area in half and continue this line around the front end to the wheel.

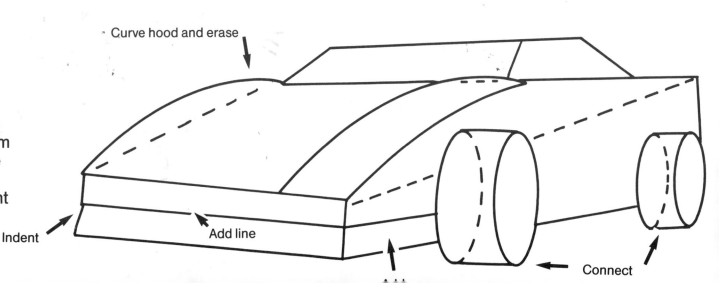

Curve hood and erase

Indent

Add line

Connect

3. Add lines and rectangles on the hood and bumper, as shown. Shape around the tires and erase the guidelines. Add lines for the window frame, door, and the spoiler at the rear.

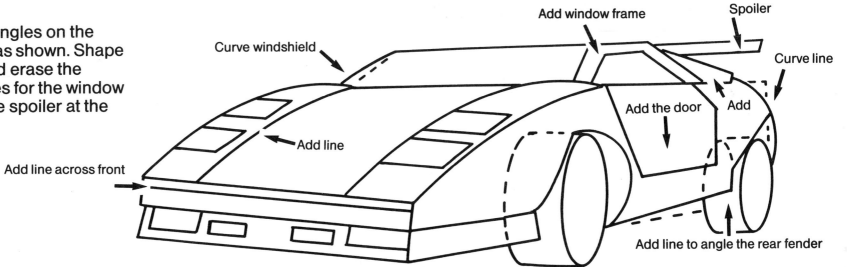

Curve windshield

Add window frame

Spoiler

Curve line

Add the door

Add

Add line

Add line across front

Add line to angle the rear fender

Hint: Draw the basic shapes lightly. These guidelines will be erased later.

4. Blend all lines to give the car a smooth, sleek look. Add final details and shading. A sideview mirror, door handle, and hubcaps complete this supercar!

Draw windshield wiper

Add details on bumper

1964 Mustang

Originally introduced at the 1964 World's Fair in New York, the Mustang was Ford's most successful model of the day—selling over 600,000 cars in its first year!

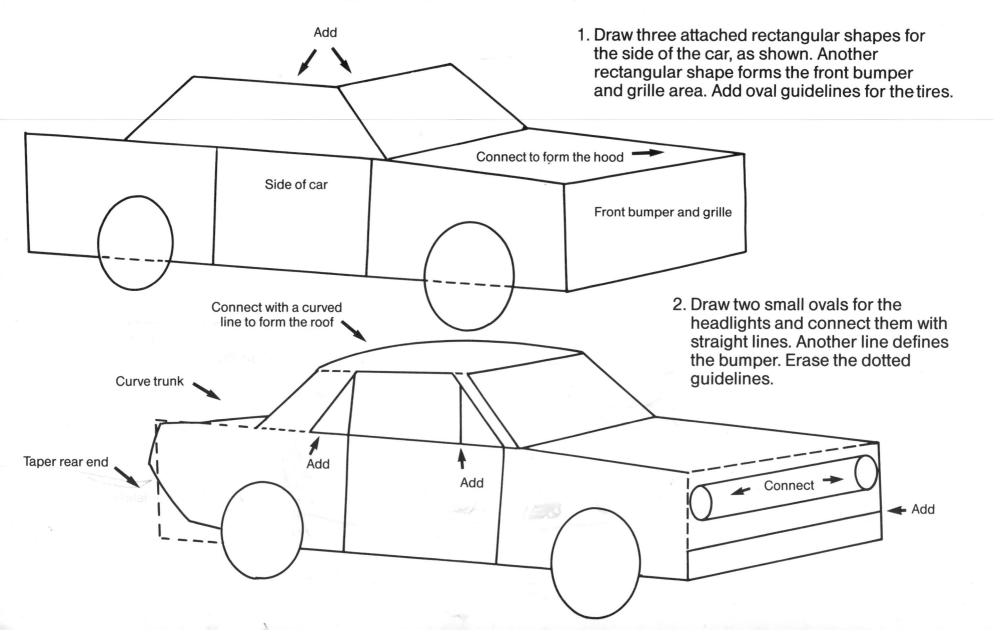

Add

1. Draw three attached rectangular shapes for the side of the car, as shown. Another rectangular shape forms the front bumper and grille area. Add oval guidelines for the tires.

Connect to form the hood →

Side of car

Front bumper and grille

Connect with a curved line to form the roof

Curve trunk

Taper rear end

Add

Add

2. Draw two small ovals for the headlights and connect them with straight lines. Another line defines the bumper. Erase the dotted guidelines.

← Connect →

← Add

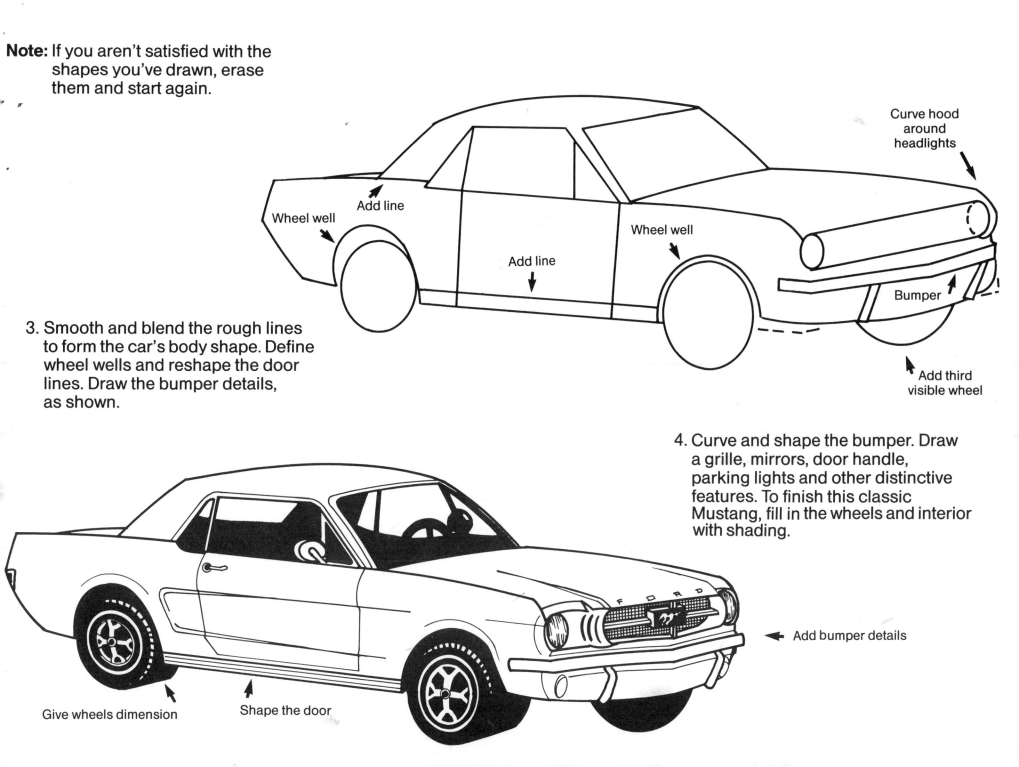

Note: If you aren't satisfied with the shapes you've drawn, erase them and start again.

Curve hood around headlights

Add line

Wheel well

Wheel well

Add line

Bumper

3. Smooth and blend the rough lines to form the car's body shape. Define wheel wells and reshape the door lines. Draw the bumper details, as shown.

Add third visible wheel

4. Curve and shape the bumper. Draw a grille, mirrors, door handle, parking lights and other distinctive features. To finish this classic Mustang, fill in the wheels and interior with shading.

FORD

Add bumper details

Give wheels dimension

Shape the door

1991 Dodge Stealth

State of the art styling makes this subcompact Dodge a dream-wish car. Aerodynamic design speeds the Stealth from 0-60 in 6 seconds.

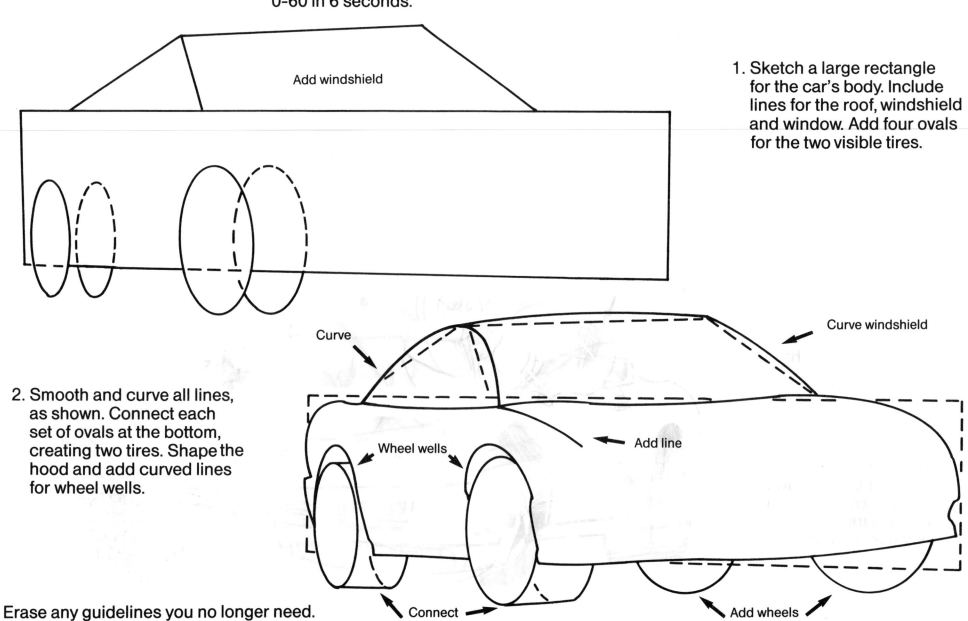

Add windshield

1. Sketch a large rectangle for the car's body. Include lines for the roof, windshield and window. Add four ovals for the two visible tires.

Curve

Curve windshield

2. Smooth and curve all lines, as shown. Connect each set of ovals at the bottom, creating two tires. Shape the hood and add curved lines for wheel wells.

Add line

Wheel wells

Connect

Add wheels

Erase any guidelines you no longer need.

Window frame

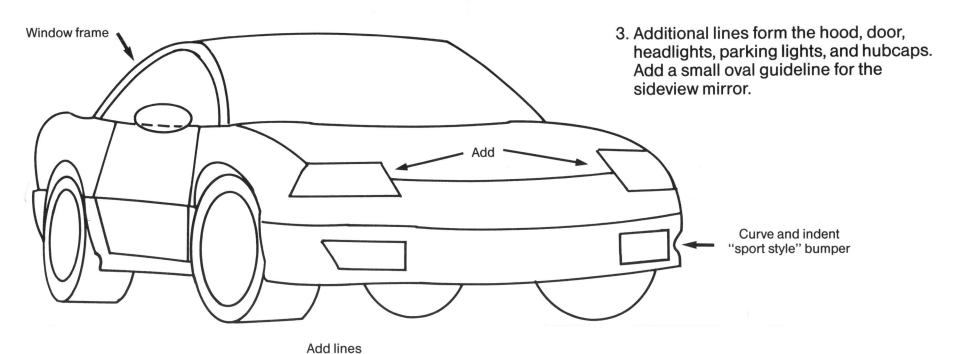

3. Additional lines form the hood, door, headlights, parking lights, and hubcaps. Add a small oval guideline for the sideview mirror.

Add

Curve and indent "sport style" bumper

Add lines to create small window

4. Draw the final details carefully. Use markers to fill in the shading on the roof, bumper details, tires and hubcaps.

Hint: For a more dramatic effect, use a thicker pen or marker for the outer shape of the car and a thin marker or pen for the inner contour lines.

Porsche 917/30

One of the most powerful sports cars ever built, this Porsche was the 1973 Can Am Champion.

Note: Be sure to extend wedge shape past top of car.

1. To draw the top and side, start with the two large shapes. Then, complete the small rectangular shape for the front bumper. Now, add other basic shapes as shown.

Rectangular shape forms top of car

Add triangle

Overlaps hood and bumper

Wedge for side

Add triangle

Front bumper

2. Next, draw two long, flowing, curved lines from the rear fins to the front fenders. Then, add lines to form the spoiler, as shown.

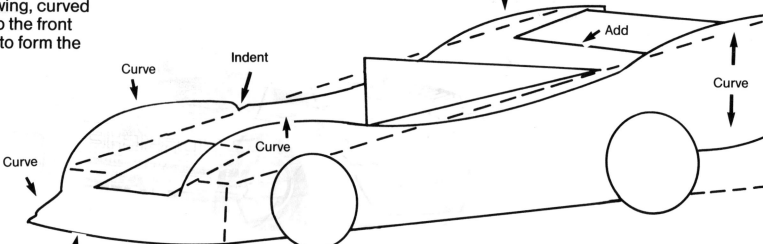

Curve

Curve

Indent

Add

Curve

Curve

Curve

Curve

Note: Take your time. If necessary, erase and start again.

3. Add contour lines to the front fenders. Draw a cylinder on the front of the car, as shown. Next, shape the wheel wells. Then, position an oval for the racer's helmet, and behind it, a wedge for the headrest.

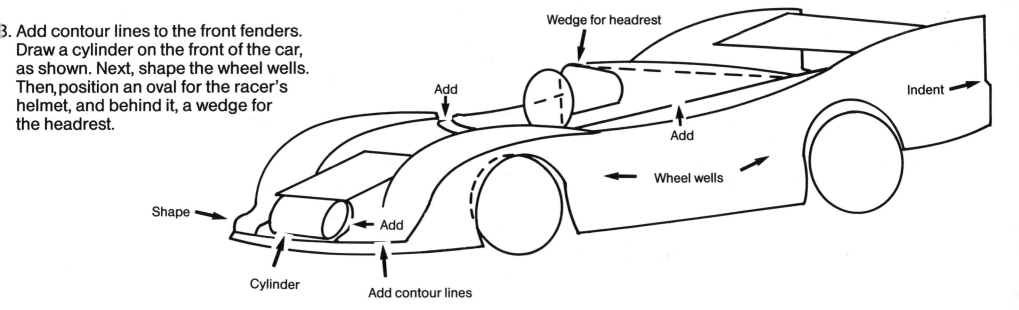

Wedge for headrest

Add

Add

Indent

Shape

Wheel wells

Cylinder

Add

Add contour lines

4. Complete this "raging rider" with vents, wheels, decals, mirrors and other details. Shade in the racer's helmet—and you're off.

Add line to spoiler

DX

PORSCHE

6

+AUDI

Add a racing number, decals and stripes

1977 Corvette Stingray

Often referred to as the all-American sports car, the Stingray is low-slung and slant-nosed for high performance and excellent handling. The 500,000th production 'Vette was sold in 1977 showing the durability of this ever-popular, distinctive design.

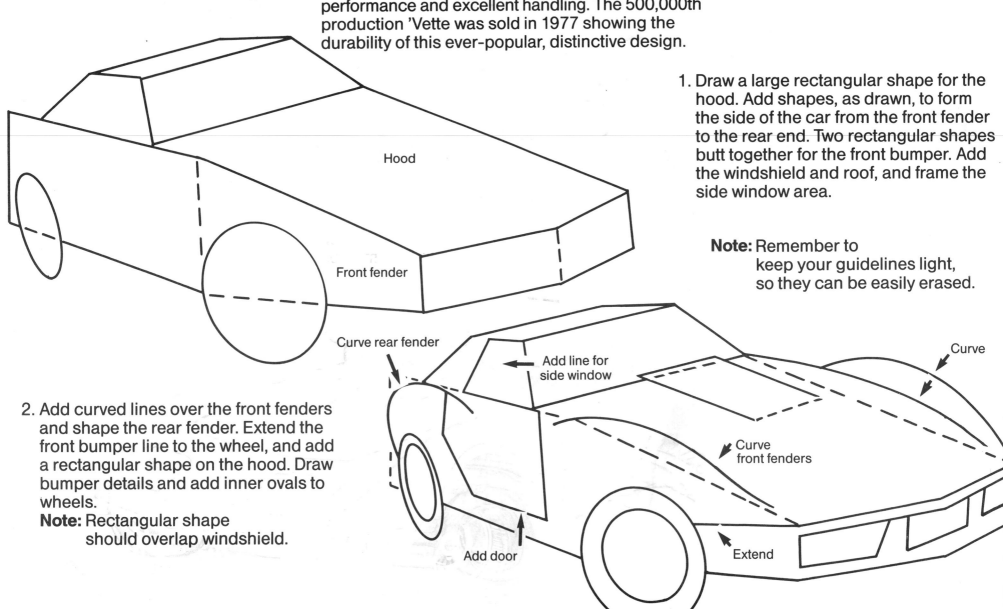

Hood

Front fender

Curve rear fender

Add line for side window

Curve

Curve front fenders

Add door

Extend

1. Draw a large rectangular shape for the hood. Add shapes, as drawn, to form the side of the car from the front fender to the rear end. Two rectangular shapes butt together for the front bumper. Add the windshield and roof, and frame the side window area.

Note: Remember to keep your guidelines light, so they can be easily erased.

2. Add curved lines over the front fenders and shape the rear fender. Extend the front bumper line to the wheel, and add a rectangular shape on the hood. Draw bumper details and add inner ovals to wheels.
Note: Rectangular shape should overlap windshield.

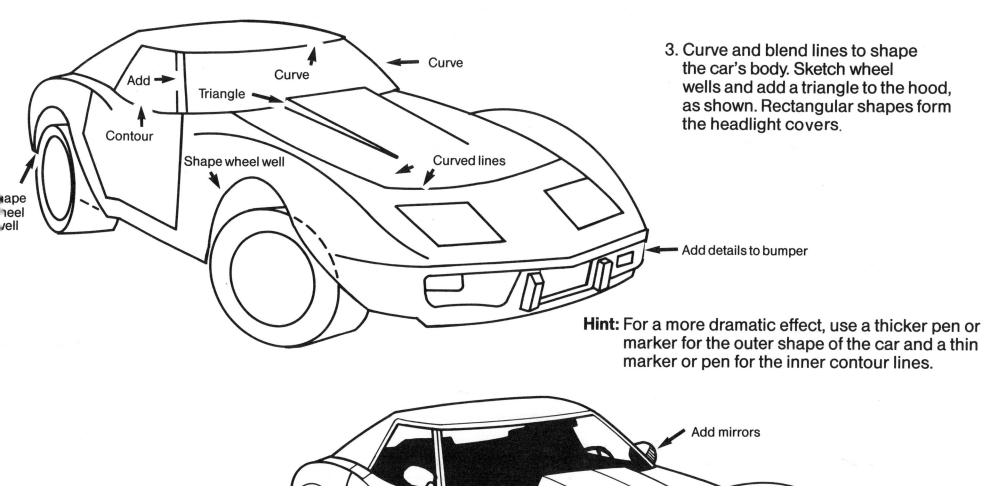

Add

Contour

Triangle

Curve

Curve

Curved lines

Shape wheel well

Shape wheel well

3. Curve and blend lines to shape the car's body. Sketch wheel wells and add a triangle to the hood, as shown. Rectangular shapes form the headlight covers.

Add details to bumper

Hint: For a more dramatic effect, use a thicker pen or marker for the outer shape of the car and a thin marker or pen for the inner contour lines.

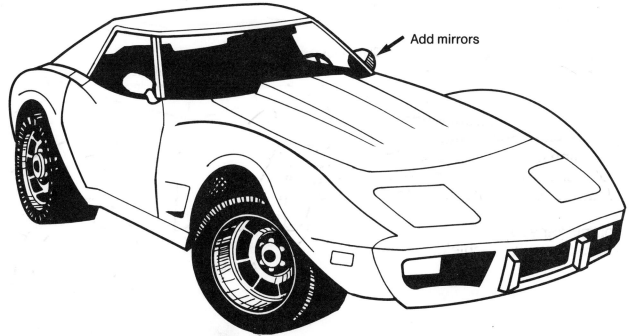

Add mirrors

Complete the Stingray by adding mirrors and other details. Add final touches by shading the interior, wheels and bumper.

1990 Crown Victoria LTD

Whether on official police business or day-to-day driving, the Crown Vic is a showcase for roomy comfortability and top-of-the-line engineering.

1. Start with basic shapes for the side, grille/bumper area and hood of the car. Add the windshield, side windows, window frames, and ovals for the wheels.

Hint: Start with the largest shape first, then add the smaller guidelines.

2. Complete the roof. Then sketch the "emergency lights" bar on top. Draw three lines across the grille/bumper area. Add a thin rectangular shape for the bumper pad, and lines for the doors.

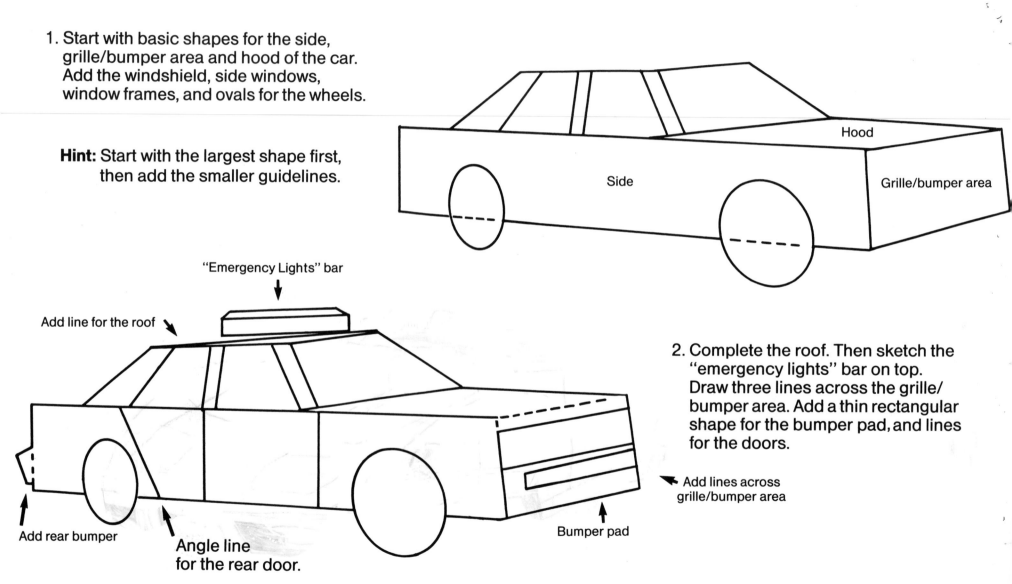

Hood

Side

Grille/bumper area

"Emergency Lights" bar

Add line for the roof

Add lines across grille/bumper area

Add rear bumper

Angle line for the rear door.

Bumper pad

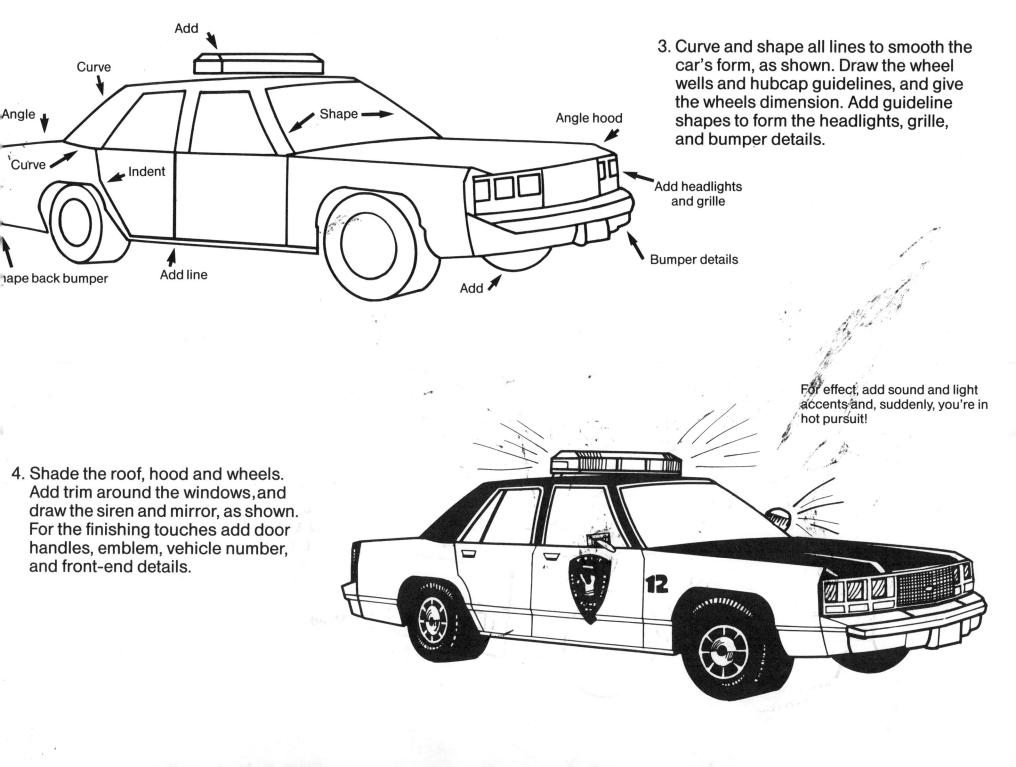

Add

Curve

Angle

Curve

Indent

Shape

Shape back bumper

Add line

Add

Angle hood

Add headlights
and grille

Bumper details

3. Curve and shape all lines to smooth the car's form, as shown. Draw the wheel wells and hubcap guidelines, and give the wheels dimension. Add guideline shapes to form the headlights, grille, and bumper details.

For effect, add sound and light accents and, suddenly, you're in hot pursuit!

4. Shade the roof, hood and wheels. Add trim around the windows, and draw the siren and mirror, as shown. For the finishing touches add door handles, emblem, vehicle number, and front-end details.

12

1955 Thunderbird

Take flight in this 2-door convertible and you'll know why the T-bird was one of the most sought after cars of its day. Its uncompromising styling set standards for years to come.

1. Draw a large, 3-dimensional rectangular shape, as shown, forming the car's body. Add lines for the door and extend them across the top. Draw ovals for the tires.

Rearview perspective

2. A wedge shape forms the special wraparound windshield—a trademark of this exciting car! Draw taillights, rear bumper and wheel wells.

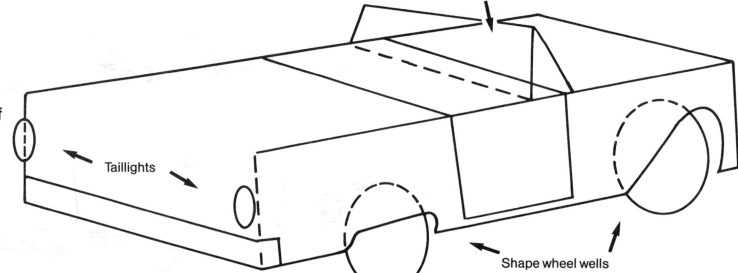

Wraparound windshield

Taillights

Shape wheel wells

. Shape and curve the car's outline. Add lines for the trunk and draw a circle to form the steering wheel. Add oval guidelines over the rear bumper and bumper details, as shown. Add dimension to the tires.

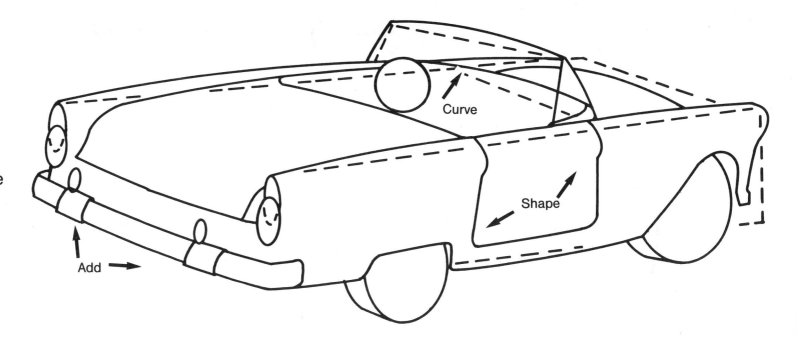

Remember: Erase and refine your lines as necessary.

. To finish this classic Thunderbird, draw all the details including body contours and dashboard.

1991 Acura NSX

The world's first all aluminum car! In a class by itself, this car's design was inspired by the F-16 jet aircraft. With a top speed of 168mph, driven by 270 horsepower, this light-weight car is no lightweight! Goes from 0-60 in 5.5 seconds.

1. Begin with a large rectangular shape butted to a wedge shape, as shown. Draw a large oval to form the roof, windshield, and windows. Add ovals for the wheels and complete the front end area.

2. Draw lines for the windows, door, and headlights. Add a small rectangle for the rear bumper.

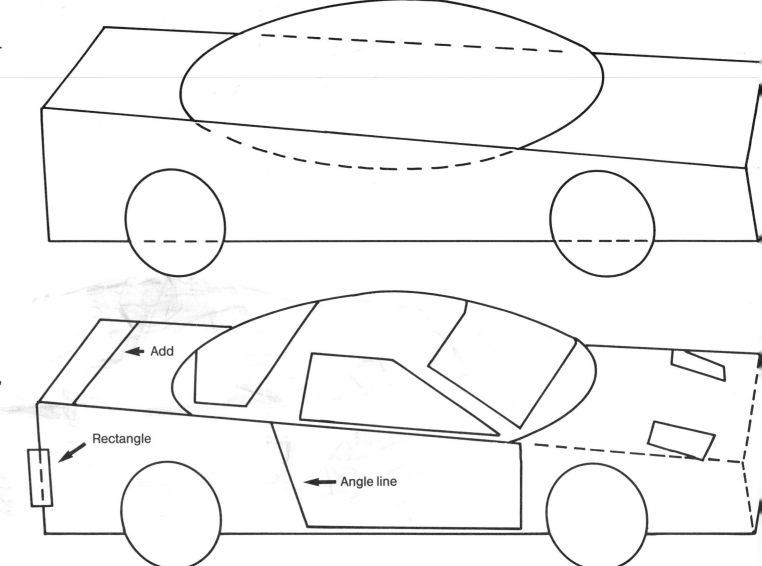

Add

Rectangle

Angle line

3. Curve and shape the outline of the car. Smooth hood
lines, and contour rear and
front bumpers.

Note: Styling the spoiler is
tricky! Take your time
to get it right. If you're
not satisfied with the
lines or shapes you've
drawn, erase them
and start again.

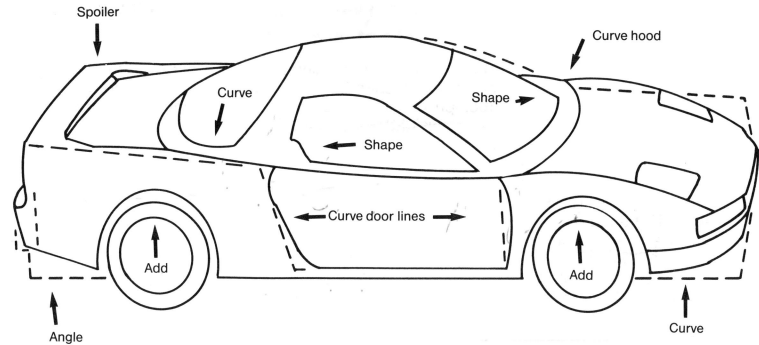

Spoiler

Curve hood

Curve

Shape

Shape

Contour bumper

Curve door lines

Add

Add

Angle

Curve

4. Add lines to refine the
windows and roof as you
shade-in details. Curved
contour lines, mirrors, hubcap details and windshield
wipers complete this high-
performance road master.

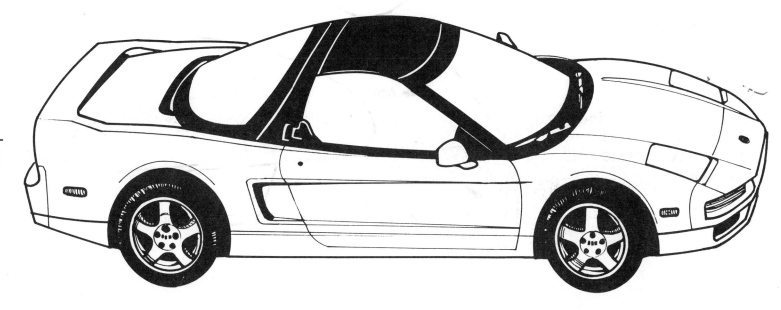

Formula 1

Able to reach speeds of nearly 200mph, the Formula 1 racing car is propelled by 450 horsepower! A slim single seater, Formula 1's are stripped to be lightning fast on straightaways—the ultimate speed machine!

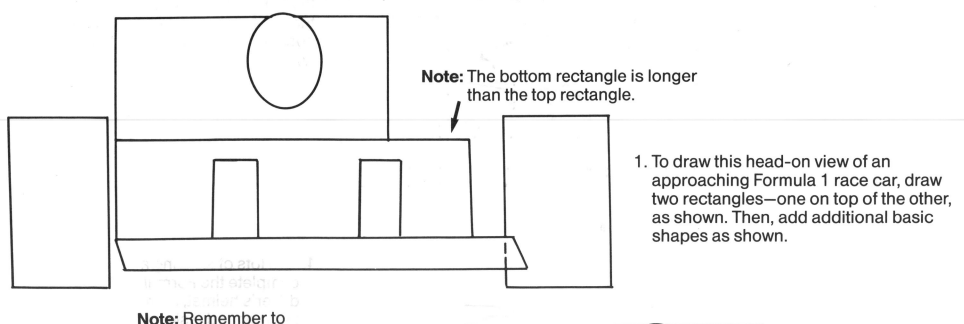

Note: The bottom rectangle is longer than the top rectangle.

1. To draw this head-on view of an approaching Formula 1 race car, draw two rectangles—one on top of the other, as shown. Then, add additional basic shapes as shown.

Note: Remember to keep your guidelines light, so they can be easily erased.

2. Draw a half-circle through the oval, and add additional basic shapes.

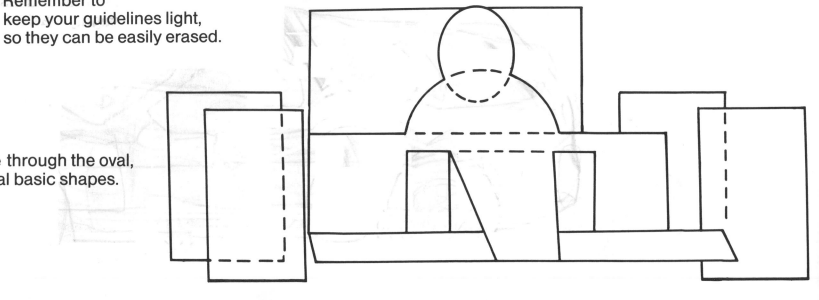

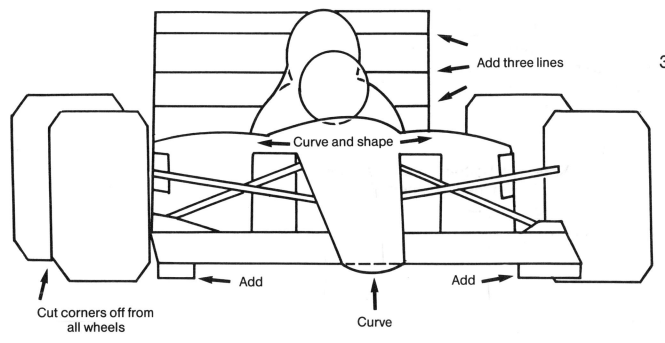

Add three lines

Curve and shape

Cut corners off from all wheels

Add

Curve

Add

3. Add crossed bars from the tires to the nose of the car. Curve the tip of the car's nose and add a circle at the top. Curve and shape the driver's cockpit. Add additional shapes, as shown.

4. Add lots of shading and details to complete the Formula 1. Draw the driver's helmet, mirrors, a racing number and insignia to identify this mighty master of the raceway!

1991 Ferrari Testarossa

Short on height—the Testarossa is only 44.5 inches high—but high on performance, this driving delight goes from 0-60 in 6.2 seconds.

1. Start by drawing three attached rectangular shapes to form the side of the car. Add other shapes for the front bumper, hood, windshield, roof, and hatchback. Add circles for the tires and lines for the door.

Remember to keep your guidelines light.

2. Draw a rectangular shape on the hood, and frame the windshield. Sketch lines to define the shape of the rear window and trunk area.

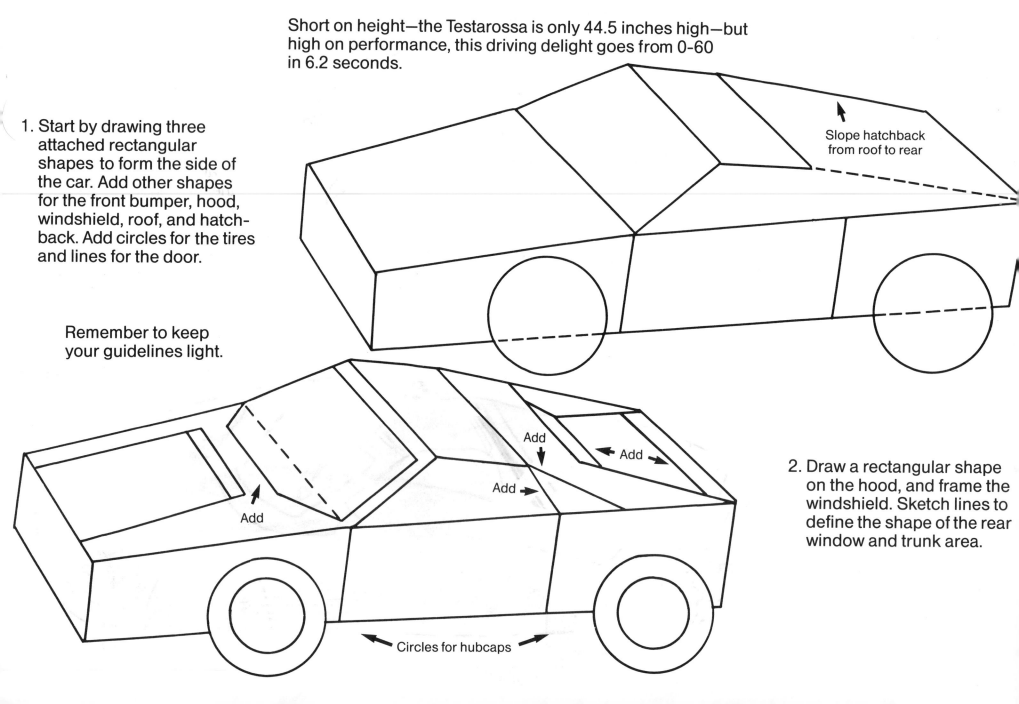

Slope hatchback from roof to rear

Add

Add

Add

Add

Add

Circles for hubcaps

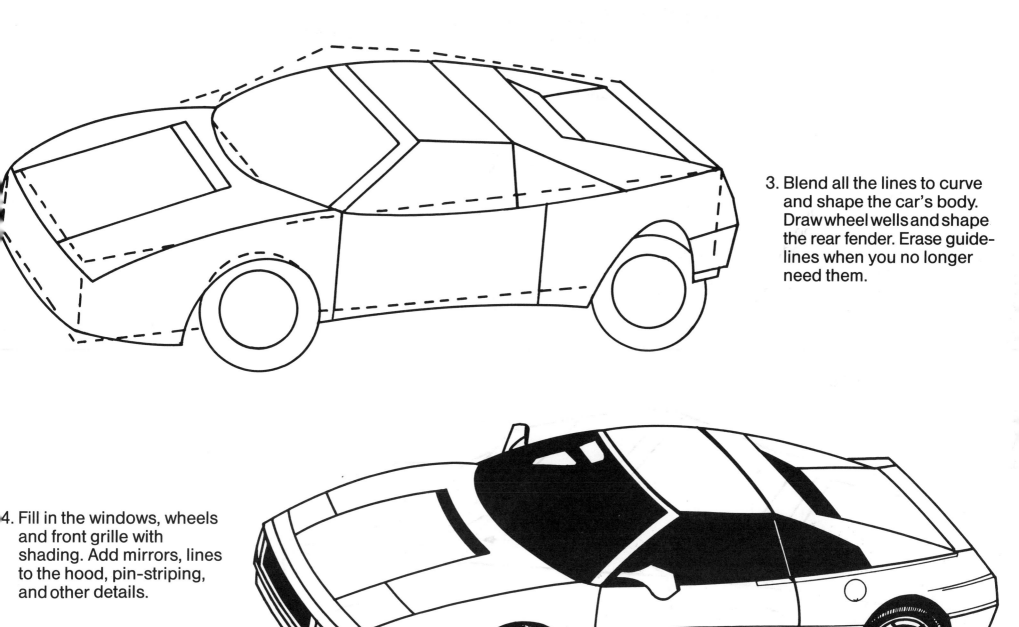

3. Blend all the lines to curve and shape the car's body. Draw wheel wells and shape the rear fender. Erase guidelines when you no longer need them.

4. Fill in the windows, wheels and front grille with shading. Add mirrors, lines to the hood, pin-striping, and other details.

1991 Nissan 300 ZX

An easy-to-handle, subcompact two-seater with flawless styling makes the Nissan a comfortable neighborhood cruiser or a hard-to-catch sports car. Reaches a top speed of 148mph and goes from 0-60 in 7.1 seconds.

1. Begin with rectangular shapes for the side and front end. Then add the additional basic shapes as shown.

2. Curve the shapes to create smooth, rounded bodylines. Frame the side window, and add the wheel wells and lines for the door.

Note: The Nissan has a rounded, curved front end.

Remember to erase the guidelines

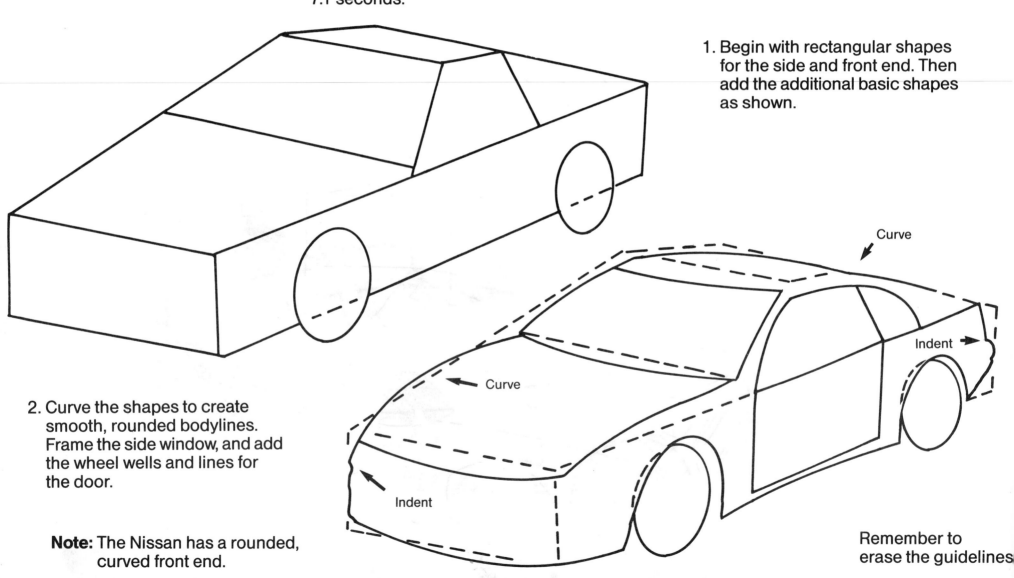

Remember to
erase the guidelines.

Add

Add

Add

Add

3. Next, blend and refine the lines outlining
   the car's shape. Add hood and bumper
   details, and dimension to the tires.
   Curve and shape the door lines, and
   carefully draw the details on the hatchback. A line across the bottom side
   panel forms the body-color molding.

4. To complete the 300ZX, add final details
   and shading.

NISSAN

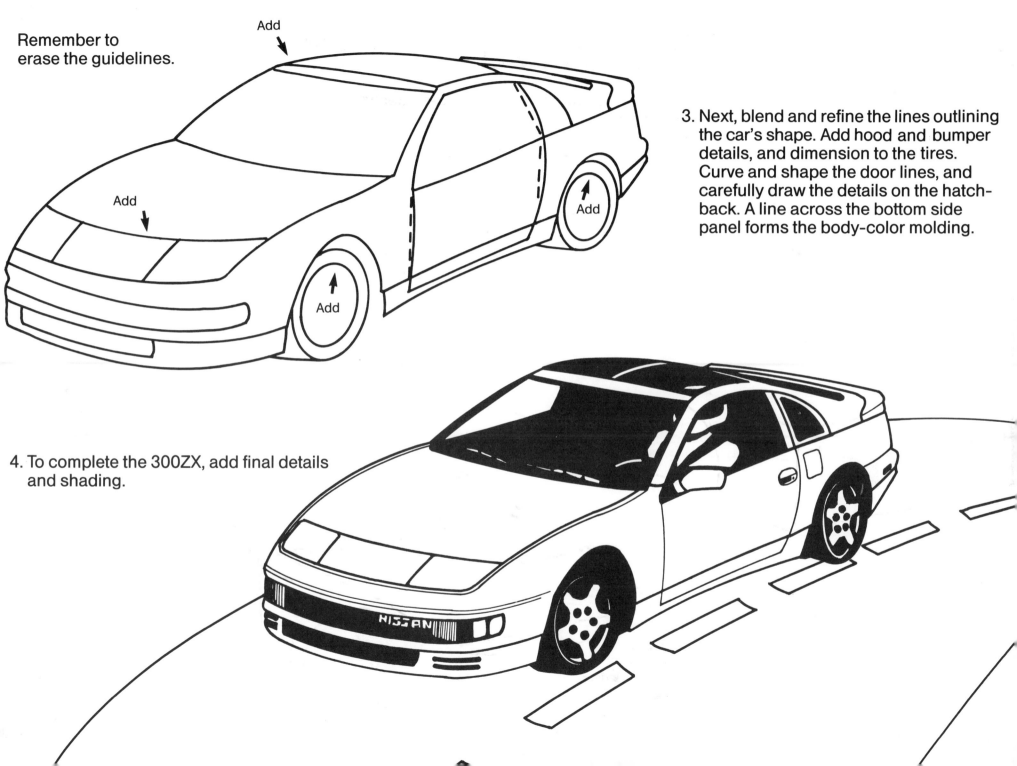

1957 Chevy Bel Air

A high performance car with a huge collector following, this top of the line Chevy had the boldest body styling of all the Bel Airs.

1. Start with rectangular shapes for the side of the car and the front bumper/grille area. Draw the windshield and side window, as shown. Add overlapping ovals for the tires.

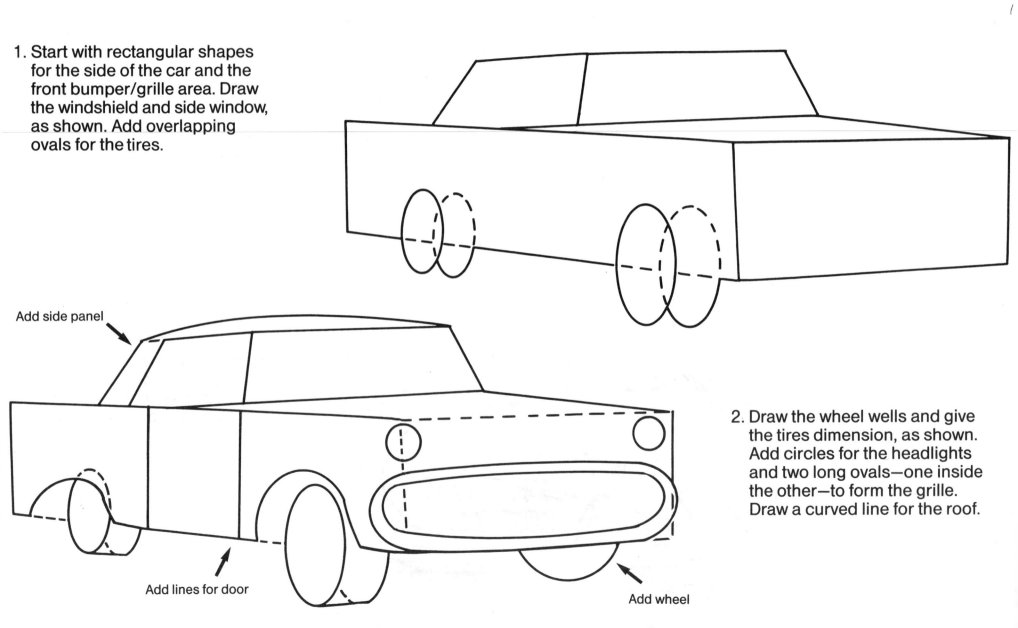

Add side panel

2. Draw the wheel wells and give the tires dimension, as shown. Add circles for the headlights and two long ovals—one inside the other—to form the grille. Draw a curved line for the roof.

Add lines for door

Add wheel

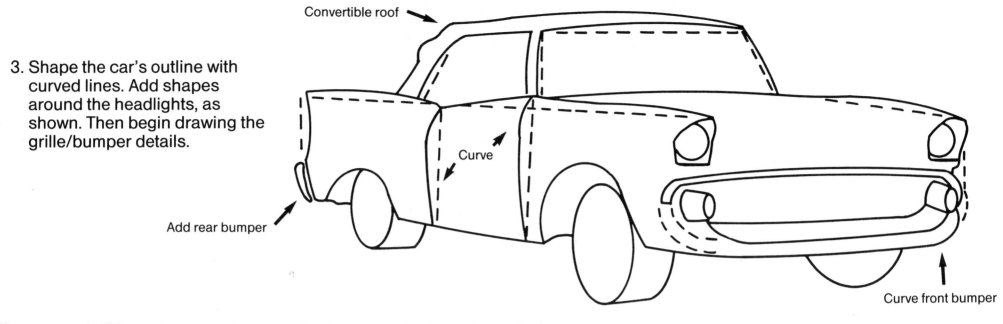

Convertible roof

3. Shape the car's outline with curved lines. Add shapes around the headlights, as shown. Then begin drawing the grille/bumper details.

Curve

Add rear bumper

Curve front bumper

Note: Erase and start again if you're not satisfied with the lines or shapes you've drawn.

4. Lastly, complete the grille and add side windows, hubcaps, door handle, and hood ornaments. Finish the Bel Air with body details and lots of shading.

Jeep Wrangler

An off-road vehicle that offers riders out-of-this-world adventure. Late models are seen as much on the main streets and highways as they are rambling around tough terrain.

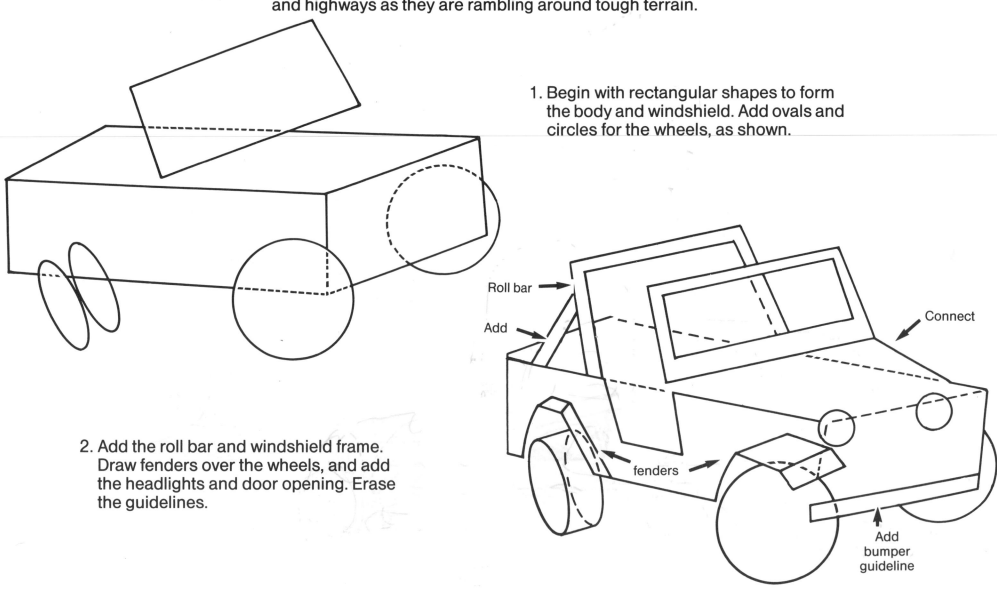

1. Begin with rectangular shapes to form the body and windshield. Add ovals and circles for the wheels, as shown.

2. Add the roll bar and windshield frame. Draw fenders over the wheels, and add the headlights and door opening. Erase the guidelines.

Roll bar

Add

Connect

fenders

Add bumper guideline

Note: It's easier to erase when your lines are lightly drawn.

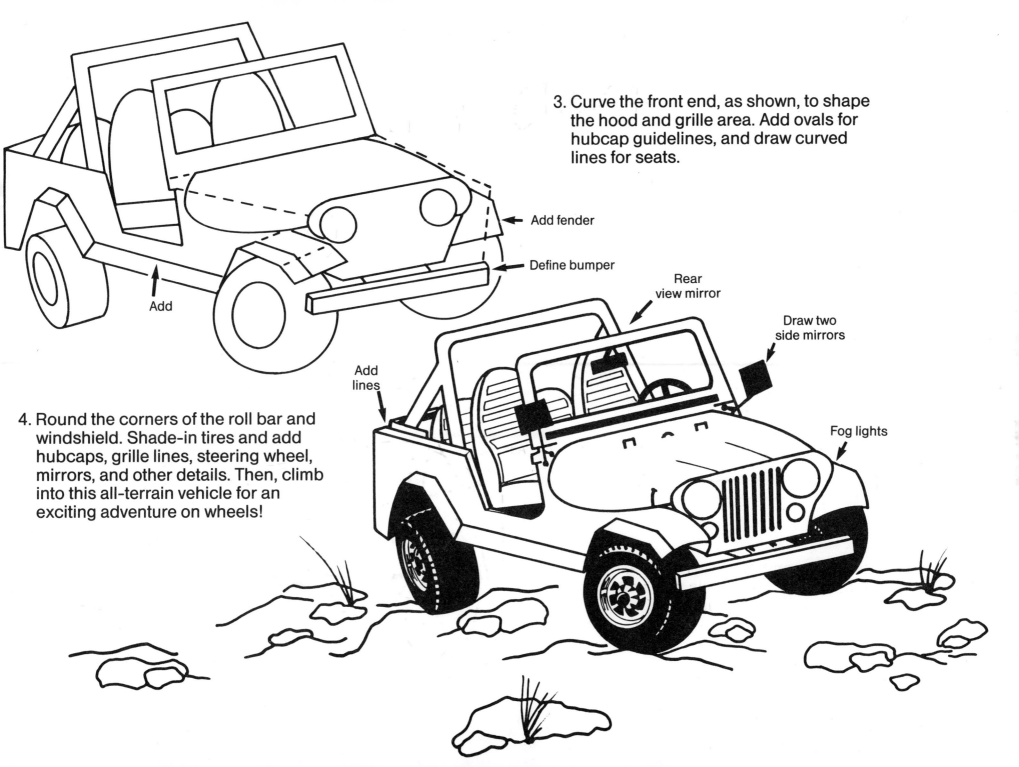

3. Curve the front end, as shown, to shape the hood and grille area. Add ovals for hubcap guidelines, and draw curved lines for seats.

Add fender

Define bumper

Add

Rear view mirror

Draw two side mirrors

Add lines

Fog lights

4. Round the corners of the roll bar and windshield. Shade-in tires and add hubcaps, grille lines, steering wheel, mirrors, and other details. Then, climb into this all-terrain vehicle for an exciting adventure on wheels!

1991 Lotus Turbo Esprit SE

This outstanding import goes from 0-60 in a head-spinning
5.1 seconds! The Lotus reaches maximum speed of 165mph.
Its 280 horsepower drives this quick-as-lightning car!

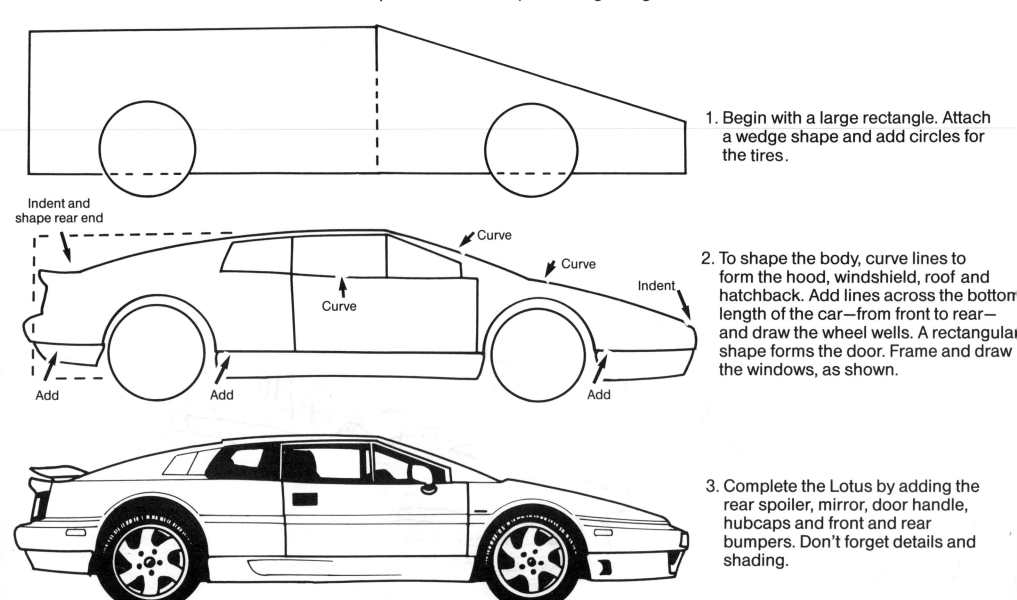

1. Begin with a large rectangle. Attach a wedge shape and add circles for the tires.

Indent and shape rear end

Curve

Curve

Curve

Indent

Add

Add

Add

2. To shape the body, curve lines to form the hood, windshield, roof and hatchback. Add lines across the bottom length of the car—from front to rear—and draw the wheel wells. A rectangular shape forms the door. Frame and draw the windows, as shown.

3. Complete the Lotus by adding the rear spoiler, mirror, door handle, hubcaps and front and rear bumpers. Don't forget details and shading.

1991 Chevy Camaro Z28

Coupe or convertible, the Camaro's windswept curves will carry you to adventure.

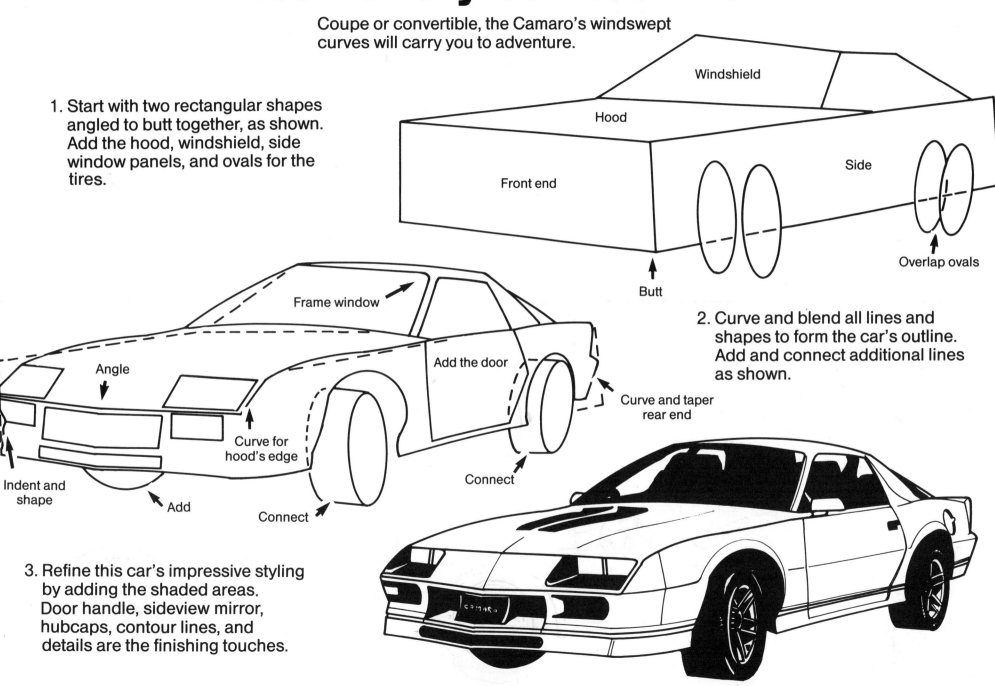

1. Start with two rectangular shapes angled to butt together, as shown. Add the hood, windshield, side window panels, and ovals for the tires.

Windshield

Hood

Side

Front end

Butt

Overlap ovals

2. Curve and blend all lines and shapes to form the car's outline. Add and connect additional lines as shown.

Frame window

Add the door

Curve and taper rear end

Angle

Curve for hood's edge

Connect

Indent and shape

Add

Connect

3. Refine this car's impressive styling by adding the shaded areas. Door handle, sideview mirror, hubcaps, contour lines, and details are the finishing touches.

CAMARO

1991 911 Porsche Turbo

With 50% more power added to the engine, the 911 reaches a top speed of 168mph and goes from 0-60 in 4.8 seconds!

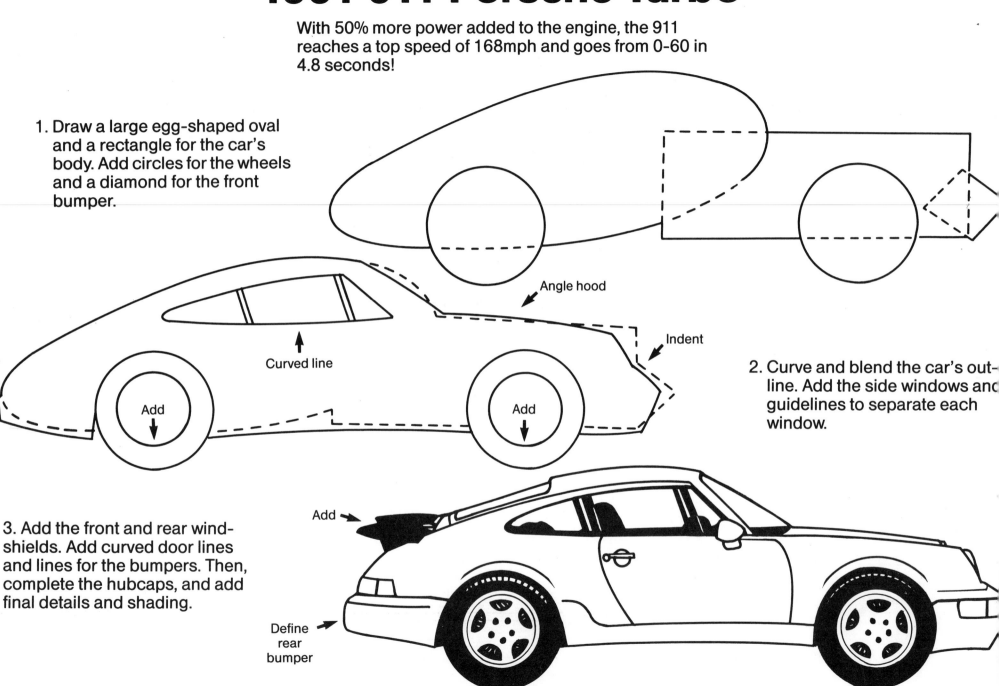

1. Draw a large egg-shaped oval and a rectangle for the car's body. Add circles for the wheels and a diamond for the front bumper.

Angle hood

Indent

Curved line

Add

Add

2. Curve and blend the car's outline. Add the side windows and guidelines to separate each window.

3. Add the front and rear windshields. Add curved door lines and lines for the bumpers. Then, complete the hubcaps, and add final details and shading.

Add

Define rear bumper

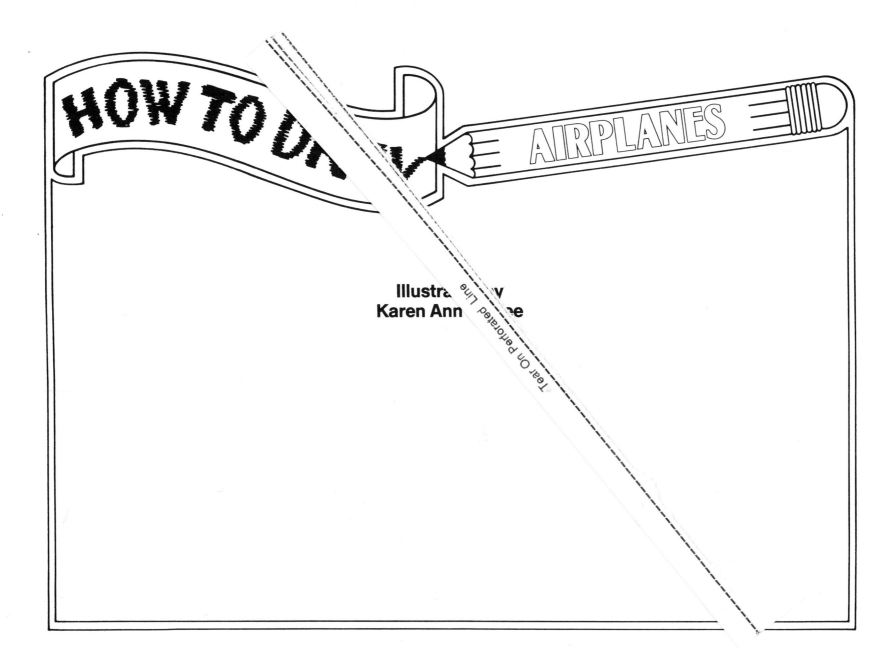

HOW TO DRAW AIRPLANES

**Illustrated by
Karen Ann Zane**

Tear On Perforated Line

P-51 MUSTANG

World War II Fighter Plane

1. **Start the P-51 with a large oval body that almost comes to a point at the nose of the plane. Add a small oval on top for the cockpit.**

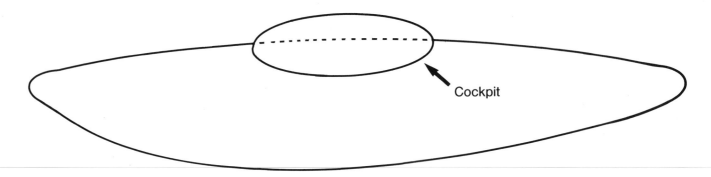

Cockpit

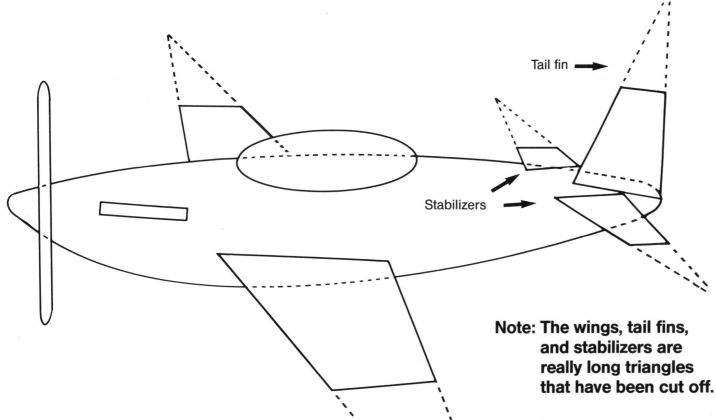

Tail fin ➡

Stabilizers ➡

2. **Next, draw the wings, tail fin, and stabilizers. Add a thin cigar-shaped oval for the propeller, and a small rectangle on the front part of the body.**

Note: The wings, tail fins, and stabilizers are really long triangles that have been cut off.

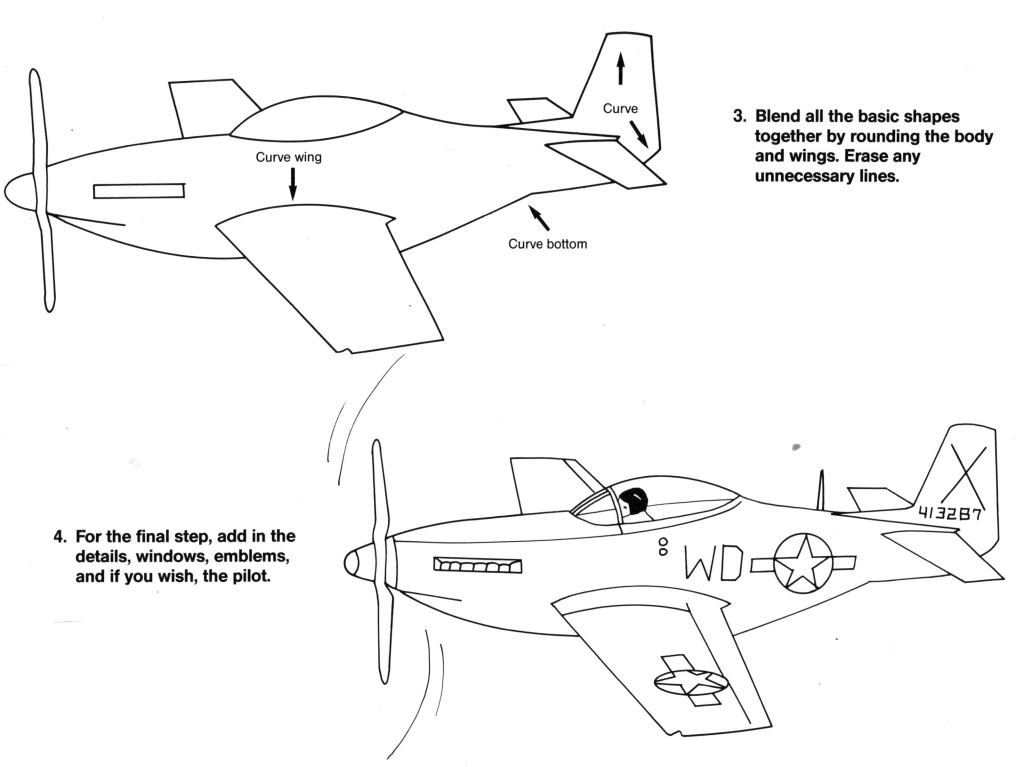

Curve

Curve wing

Curve bottom

3. **Blend all the basic shapes together by rounding the body and wings. Erase any unnecessary lines.**

4. **For the final step, add in the details, windows, emblems, and if you wish, the pilot.**

413287

WD

CONCORDE

1. **Draw a long oval, pointed at both ends, for the body. Then add a large triangle for the wings.**

2. **At the bottom of each wing add four small rectangular shapes.**

Note: Always draw guidelines lightly. If you don't like the way something looks, erase and try again.

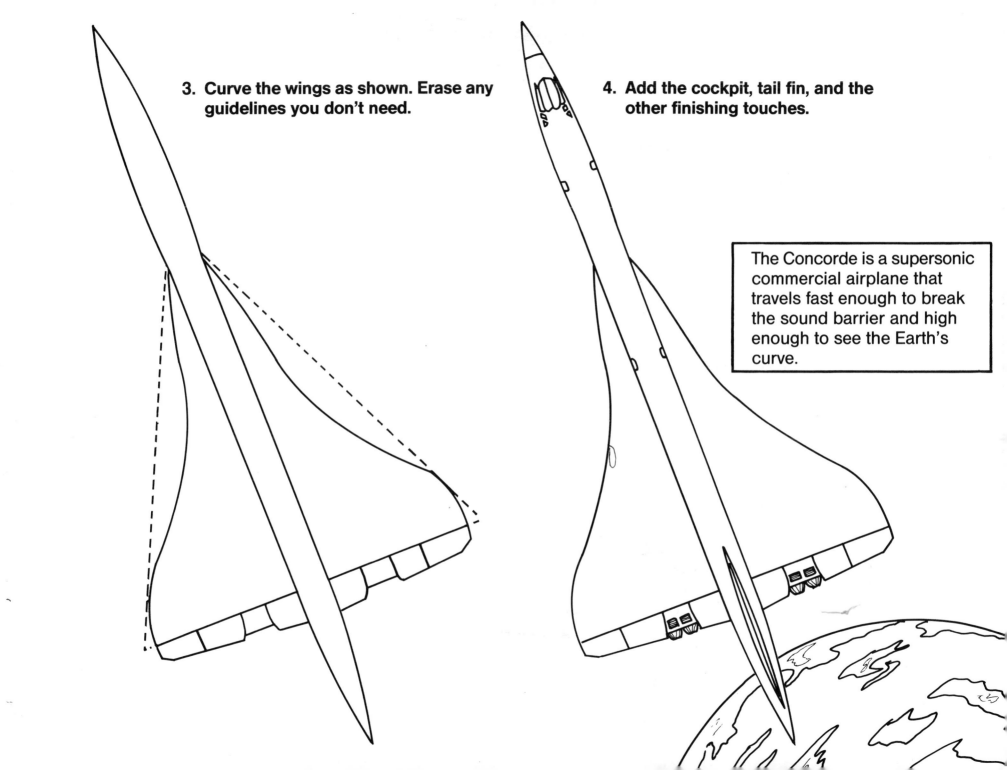

3. Curve the wings as shown. Erase any guidelines you don't need.

4. Add the cockpit, tail fin, and the other finishing touches.

The Concorde is a supersonic commercial airplane that travels fast enough to break the sound barrier and high enough to see the Earth's curve.

SR-71 BLACKBIRD

The SR-71 is a long-range
reconnaissance plane whose speed
exceeds Mach 3 (2,500 mph).

1. **Start your drawing with a large oval,
   pointed at the front end. Add the
   rectangles and smaller ovals. It's easy to
   draw anything when you break it down
   into simple shapes!**

2. **Draw circles on the front of the turbo jets.
   Inside each circle draw a small triangle.
   Then add triangles to the sides of the
   turbo jets. Don't forget the tail fins.**

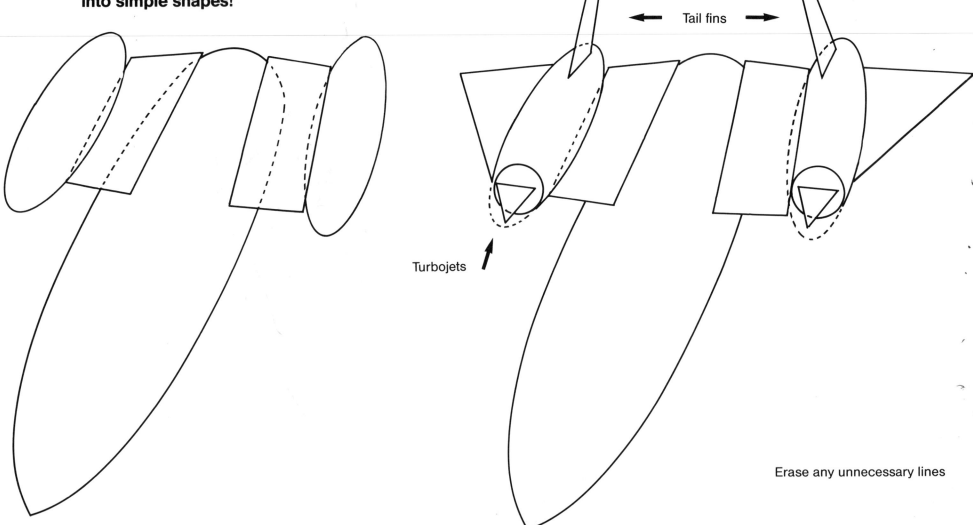

Tail fins

Turbojets

Erase any unnecessary lines

3. Add a rounded-off oval down the center of the plane. Blend all shapes together until you have a clean, line drawing.

4. Finish the SR-71 by adding details. Create a background by adding clouds.

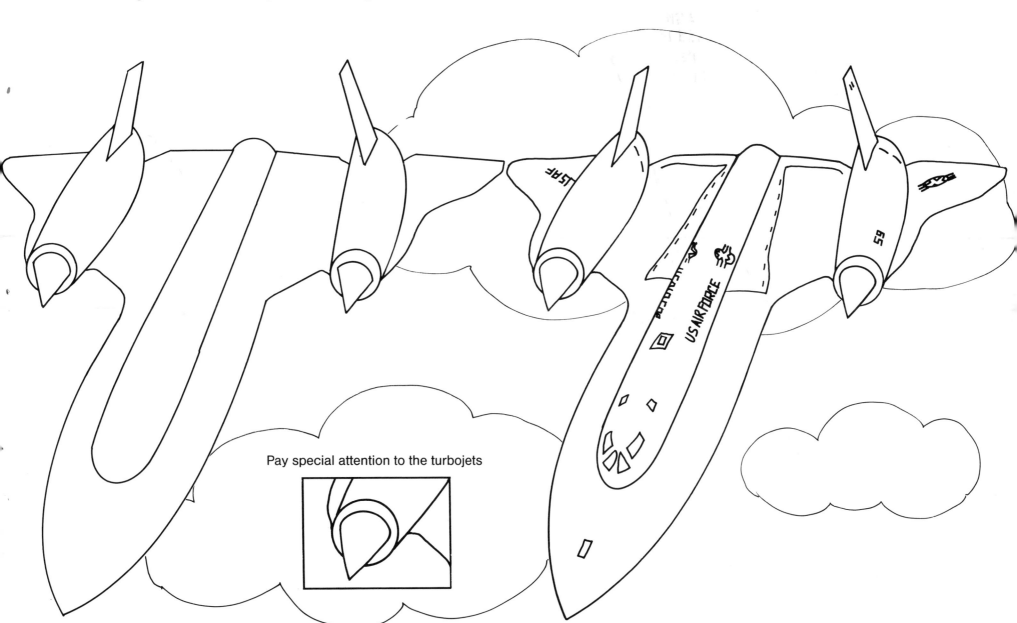

Pay special attention to the turbojets

F-18 HORNET

Navy fighter and light attack bomber

1. Lightly draw an oval, pointed at both ends, and smaller ovals on each side.

Triangle →

Note: Always draw the largest shape first, then the smaller ones.

2. Add the wings, tail fins, stabilizers, and an oval for the cockpit. Use basic shapes as your guidelines.

3. Connect the wings as shown. Blend the guidelines into the F-18 shape. Erase any lines you no longer need.

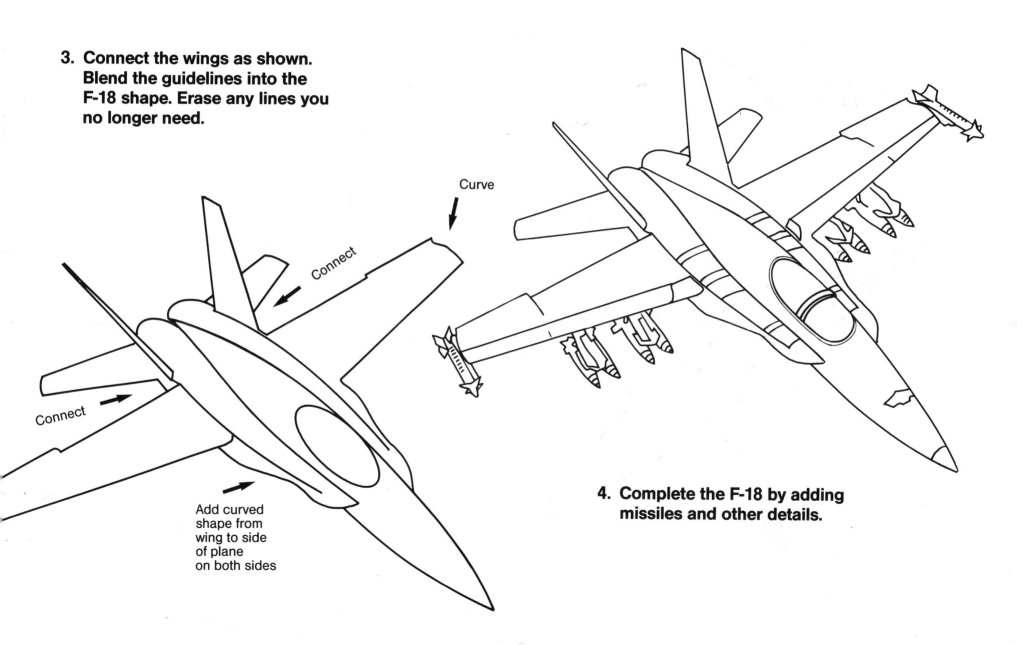

Curve

Connect

Connect

Add curved shape from wing to side of plane on both sides

4. Complete the F-18 by adding missiles and other details.

STEALTH BOMBER

Due to its unique "boomerang" shape and its ability to fly slowly at low altitudes, it is almost impossible for radar to detect the Stealth Bomber.

1. Begin your drawing with a large triangle. Add three small triangles on the bottom and an oval on top.

2. Extend wings on both sides of triangle and add additional lines as shown. Keep your guidelines light.

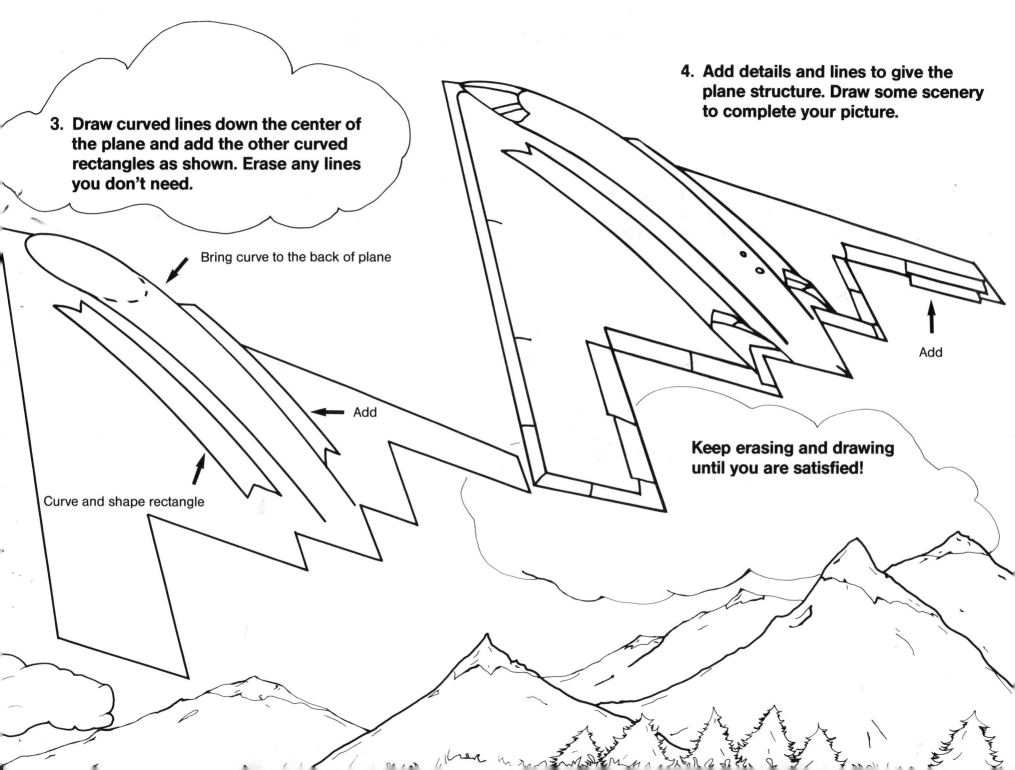

3. Draw curved lines down the center of the plane and add the other curved rectangles as shown. Erase any lines you don't need.

Bring curve to the back of plane

Add

Curve and shape rectangle

4. Add details and lines to give the plane structure. Draw some scenery to complete your picture.

Add

Keep erasing and drawing until you are satisfied!

THE SPIRIT OF ST. LOUIS

In 1927 Charles Lindbergh, in this
plane, was the first person to fly alone,
nonstop, across the Atlantic.

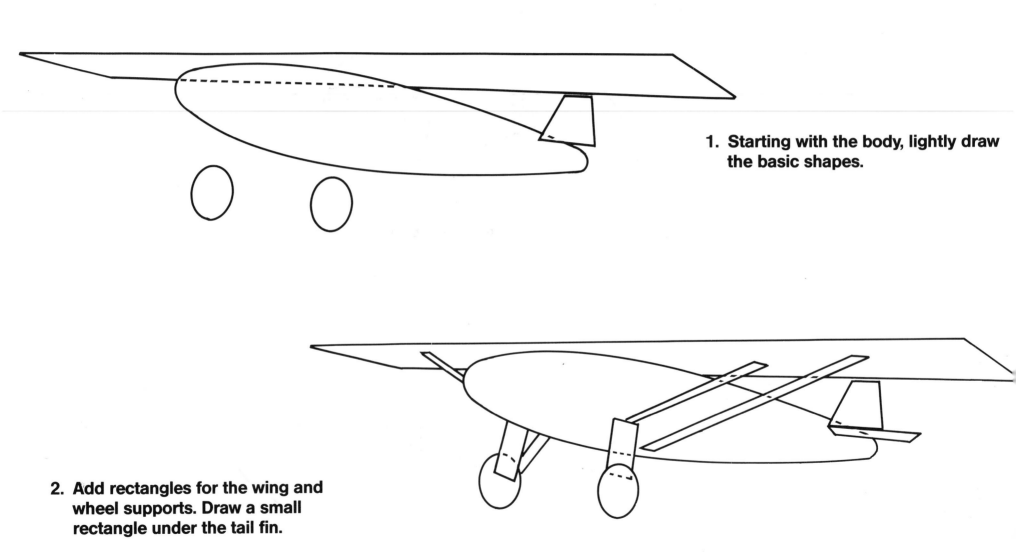

1. **Starting with the body, lightly draw the basic shapes.**

2. **Add rectangles for the wing and wheel supports. Draw a small rectangle under the tail fin.**

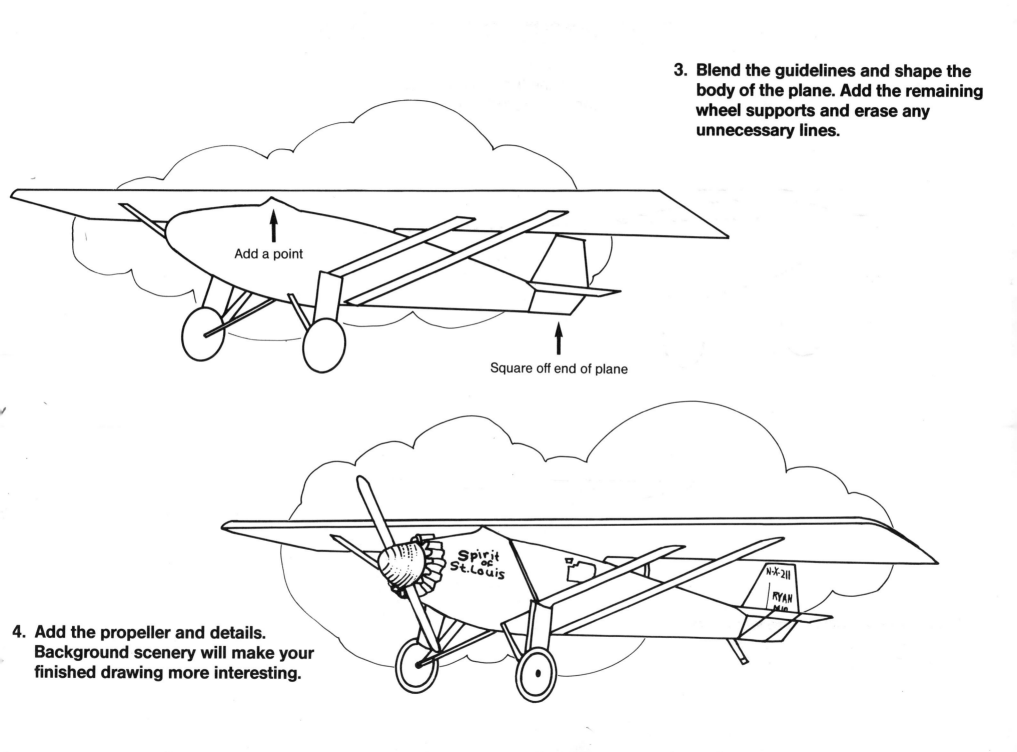

3. **Blend the guidelines and shape the body of the plane. Add the remaining wheel supports and erase any unnecessary lines.**

Add a point

Square off end of plane

4. **Add the propeller and details. Background scenery will make your finished drawing more interesting.**

Spirit of St. Louis

N-X-211

RYAN

MIRAGE 2000

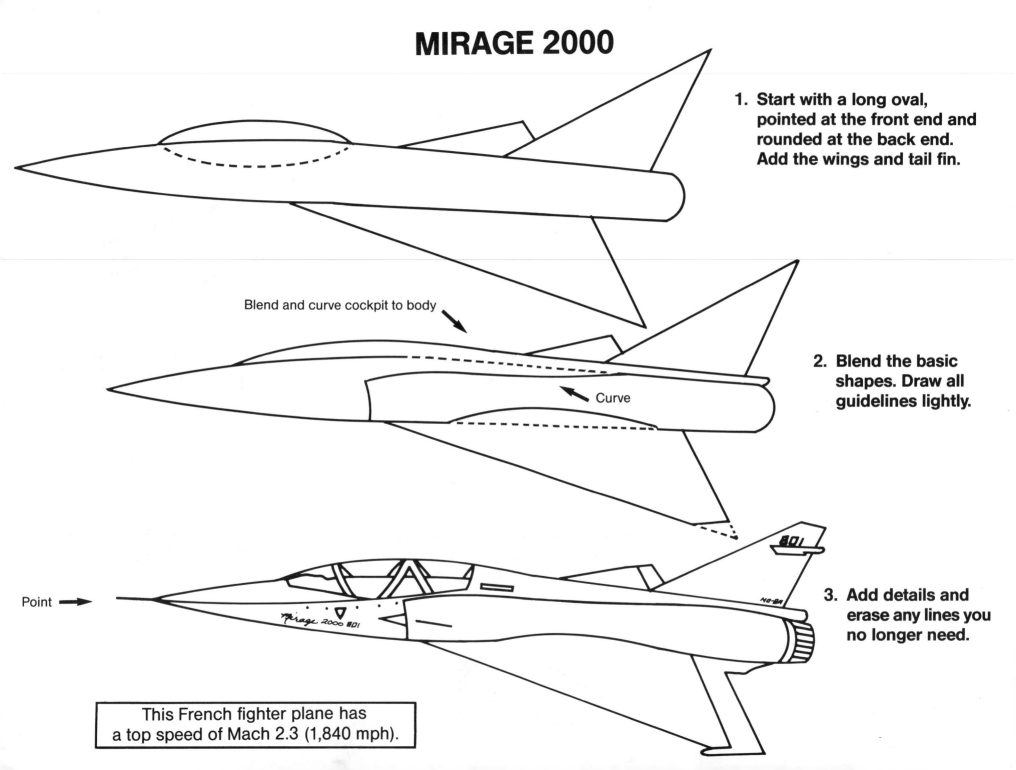

1. **Start with a long oval, pointed at the front end and rounded at the back end. Add the wings and tail fin.**

Blend and curve cockpit to body

Curve

2. **Blend the basic shapes. Draw all guidelines lightly.**

Point ➤

3. **Add details and erase any lines you no longer need.**

This French fighter plane has a top speed of Mach 2.3 (1,840 mph).

SPACE SHUTTLE

The shuttle blasts off like
a rocket, but returns to Earth,
landing like an airplane
on a long runway.

. **Begin by drawing the basic
shapes. These are only
guidelines so draw them
lightly.**

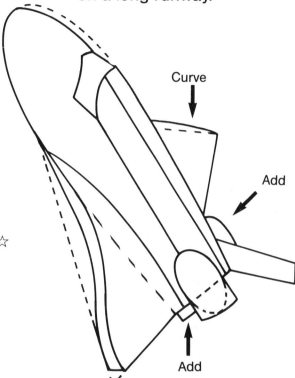

Curve

Add

Add

2. **Add the cockpit and additional
lines. Curve the wings and
blend all the shapes. Erase all
guidelines.**

Square-off oval as shown

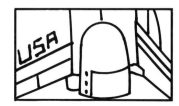

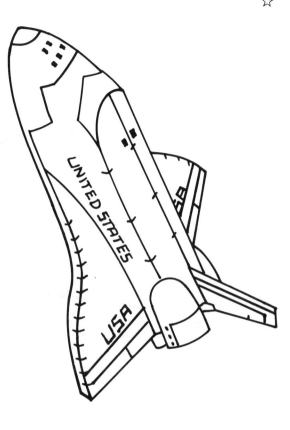

3. **Finish your drawing by adding
details and emblems.**

UNITED STATES

USA

BOEING 747

This huge commercial
jet can fly over 600 miles
per hour and carry
500 passengers.

**1. Begin with basic shapes
for the body and wings.
Remember to draw all
guidelines lightly.**

**2. Add the cockpit,
stabilizers, and a triangle
at the bottom of the
plane's body.**

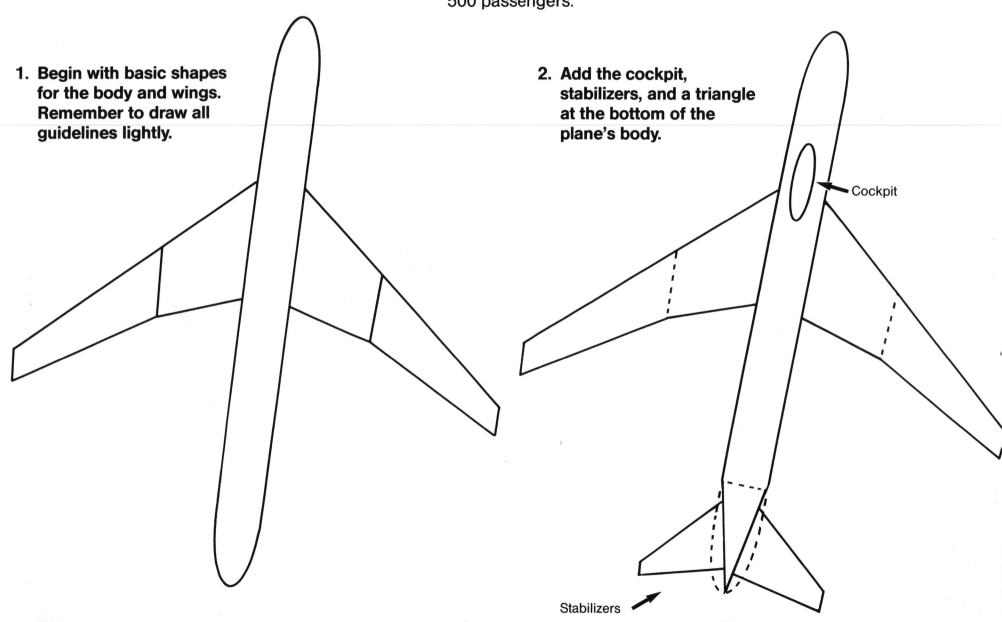

Cockpit

Stabilizers

3. Curve the back end of the body and extend lines at the wing tips. Erase guidelines.

4. To finish the 747, add the engines, tail fin, and details.

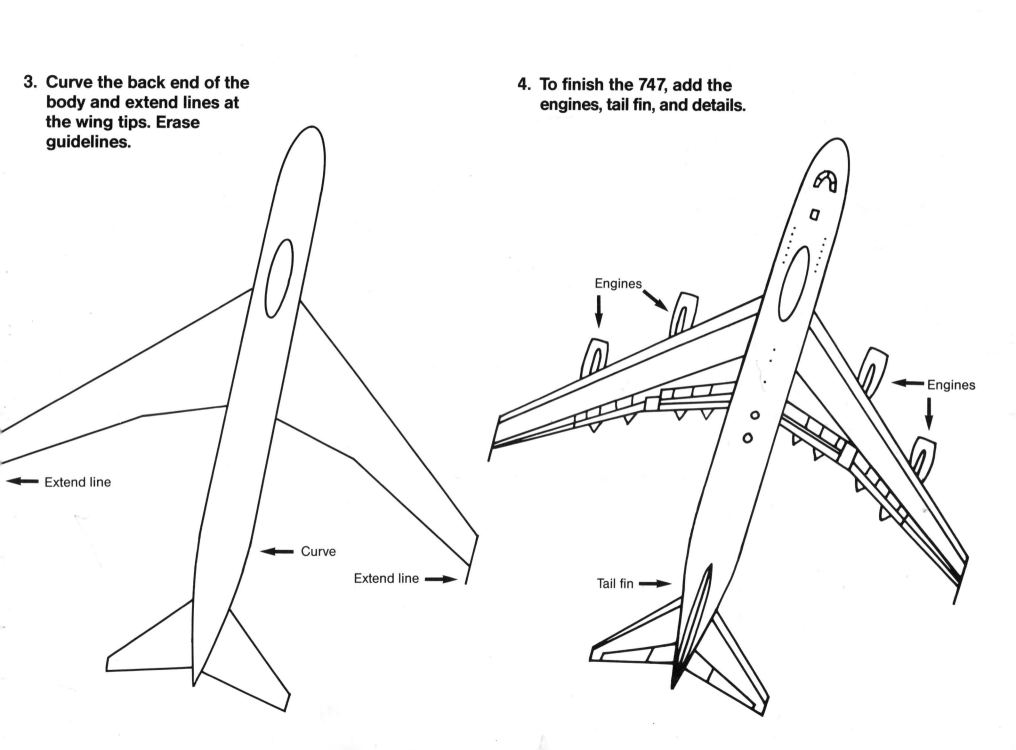

← Extend line

← Curve

Extend line →

Engines

Engines

Tail fin →

B-1B BOMBER

United States strategic
heavy bomber

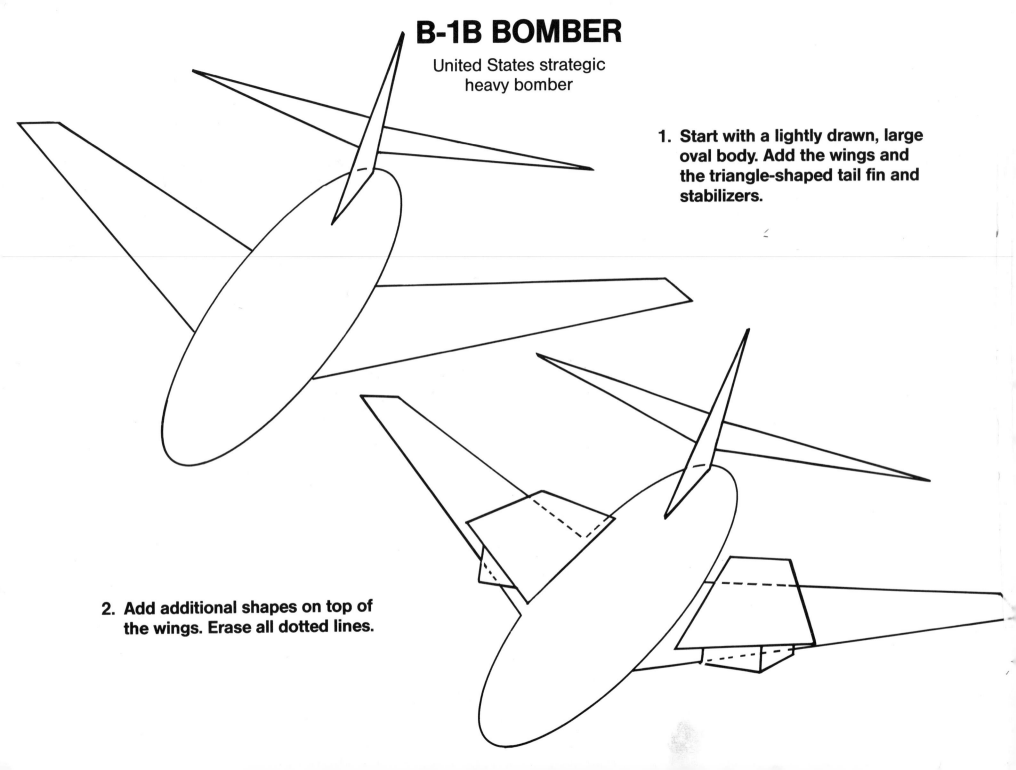

1. **Start with a lightly drawn, large oval body. Add the wings and the triangle-shaped tail fin and stabilizers.**

2. **Add additional shapes on top of the wings. Erase all dotted lines.**

Curve

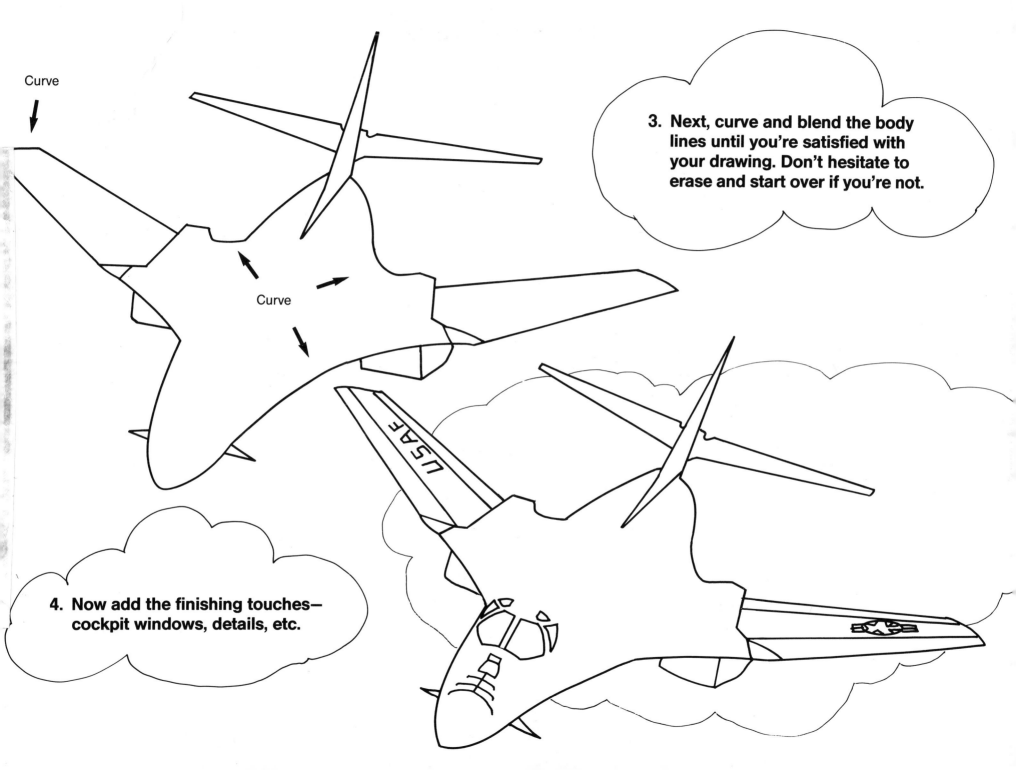

Curve

3. Next, curve and blend the body lines until you're satisfied with your drawing. Don't hesitate to erase and start over if you're not.

4. Now add the finishing touches— cockpit windows, details, etc.

USAF

HAWKER TYPHOON

World War II British
fighter plane

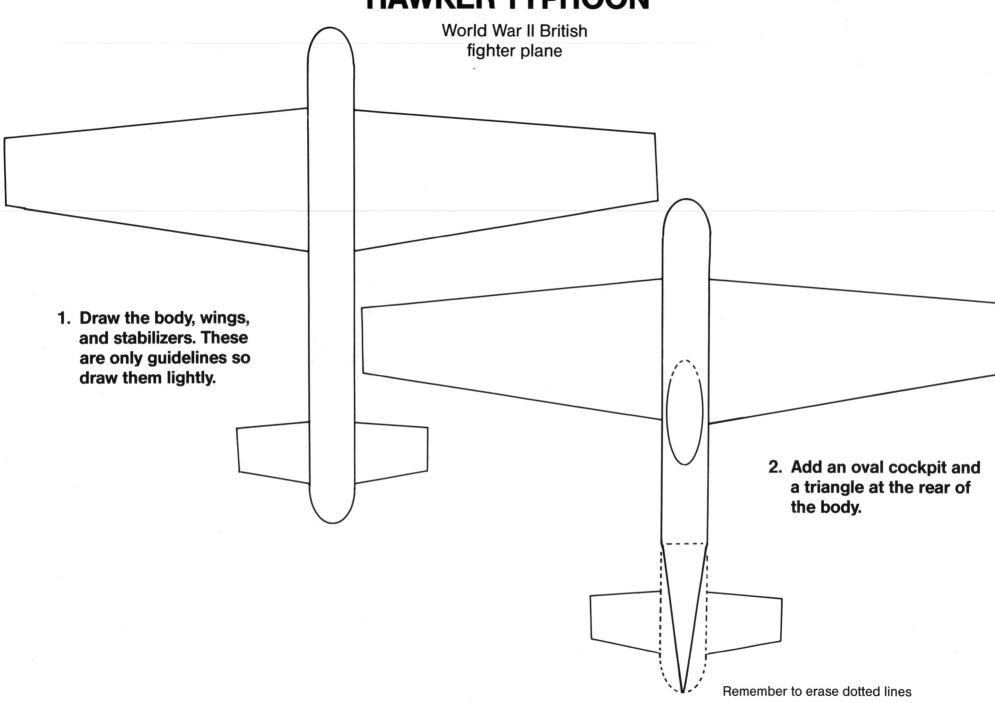

1. **Draw the body, wings, and stabilizers. These are only guidelines so draw them lightly.**

2. **Add an oval cockpit and a triangle at the rear of the body.**

Remember to erase dotted lines

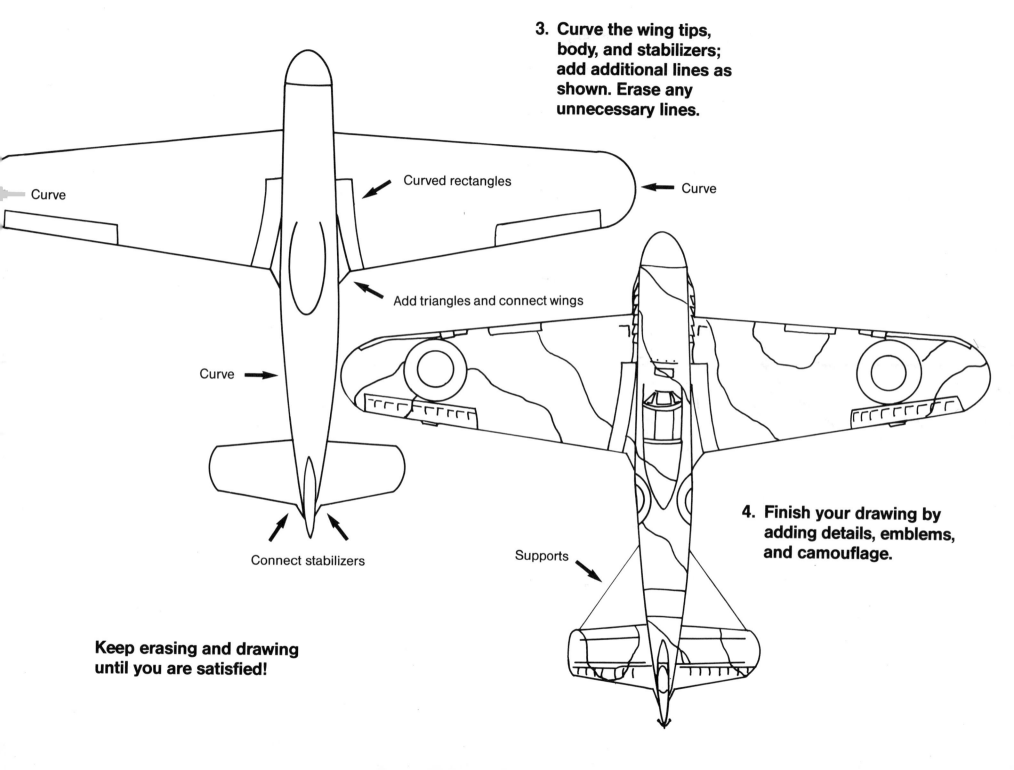

3. Curve the wing tips, body, and stabilizers; add additional lines as shown. Erase any unnecessary lines.

Curved rectangles

Curve

Curve

Add triangles and connect wings

Curve

Connect stabilizers

Supports

4. Finish your drawing by adding details, emblems, and camouflage.

Keep erasing and drawing until you are satisfied!

FB-111

Known as the "Aardvark"
because of its long, droopy,
radar-filled snout.

1. **Start by lightly drawing the basic body shapes.**

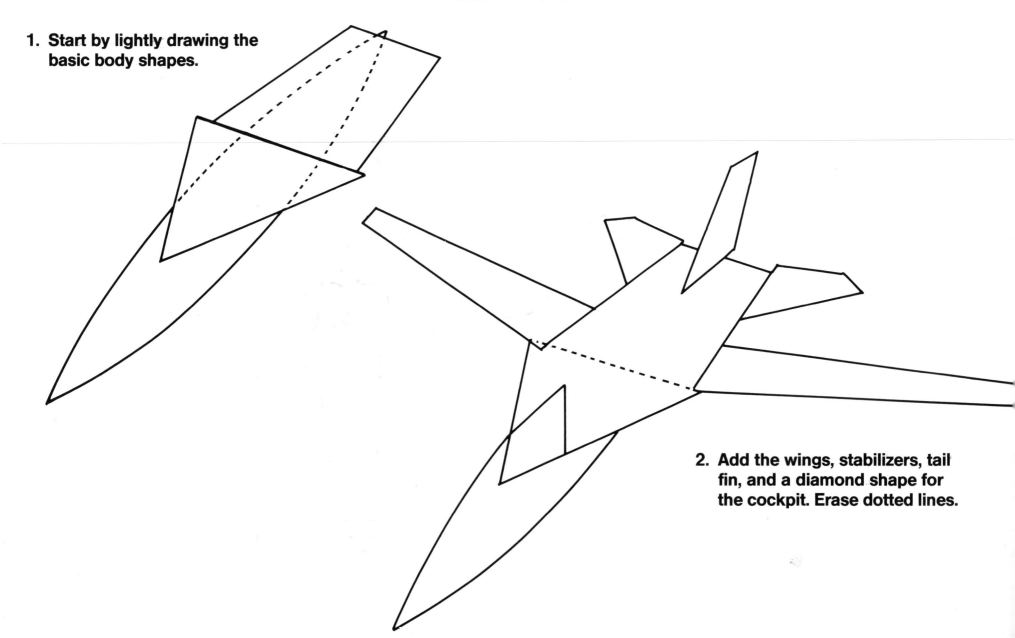

2. **Add the wings, stabilizers, tail fin, and a diamond shape for the cockpit. Erase dotted lines.**

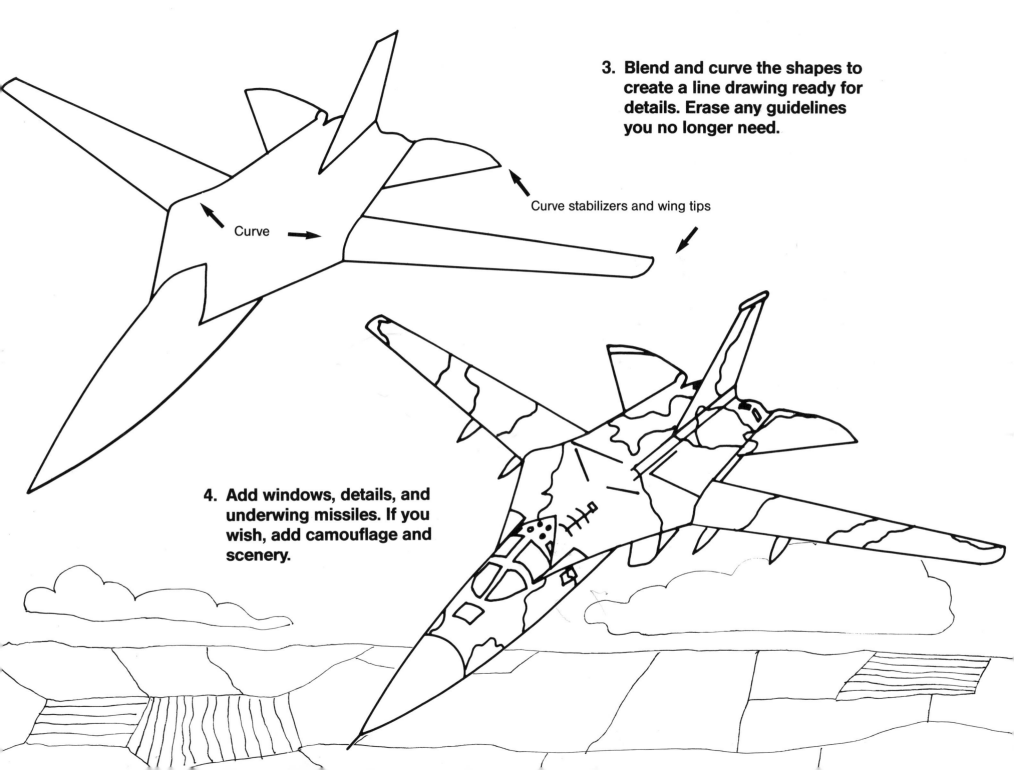

3. Blend and curve the shapes to create a line drawing ready for details. Erase any guidelines you no longer need.

Curve stabilizers and wing tips

Curve

4. Add windows, details, and underwing missiles. If you wish, add camouflage and scenery.

BRITISH SEA HARRIER

The Harrier jump-jet is a VTOL
(Vertical Takeoff And Landing) fighter plane.

1. **Draw the basic body shape. Add triangles for the wings and stabilizers. Draw guideline shapes lightly.**

2. **Add squares and rectangles on body, and ovals under the wings.**

Cut off ends of triangles ➞

Add triangles on both sides

Remember to erase dotted lines

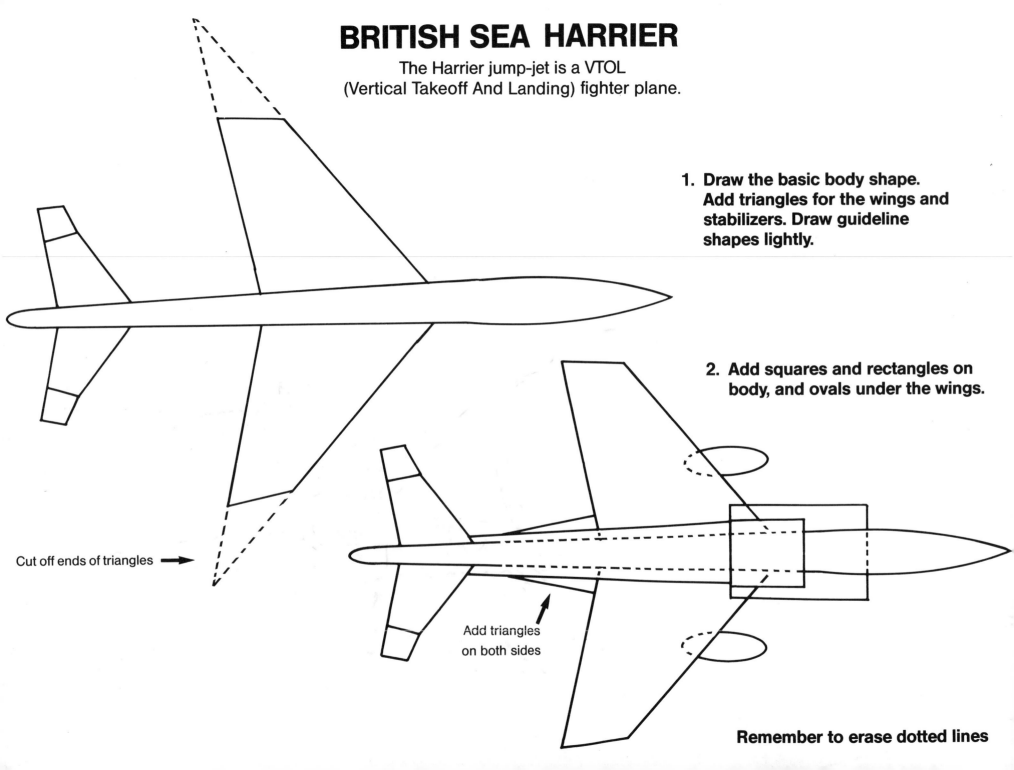

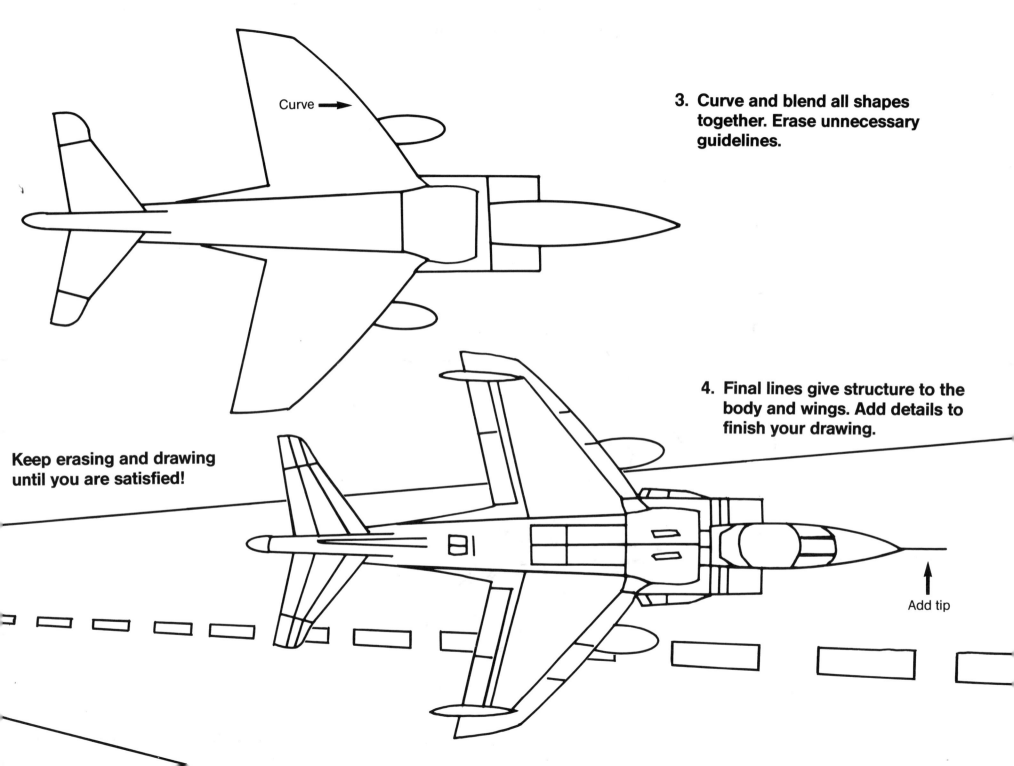

Curve ⟶

3. Curve and blend all shapes together. Erase unnecessary guidelines.

4. Final lines give structure to the body and wings. Add details to finish your drawing.

Keep erasing and drawing until you are satisfied!

Add tip

AH-64 APACHE HELICOPTER

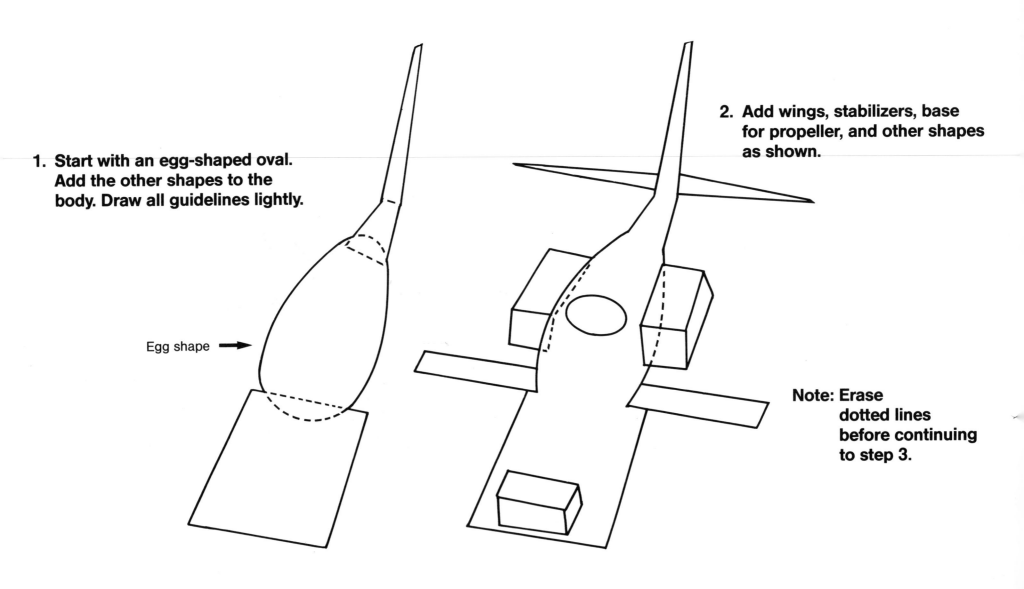

1. **Start with an egg-shaped oval. Add the other shapes to the body. Draw all guidelines lightly.**

Egg shape ➔

2. **Add wings, stabilizers, base for propeller, and other shapes as shown.**

Note: Erase dotted lines before continuing to step 3.

3. Connect, curve, and blend all lines until you're satisfied. Don't hesitate to erase and start over.

4. Complete the Apache by adding the underwing missiles, motion for the propeller, and other details.

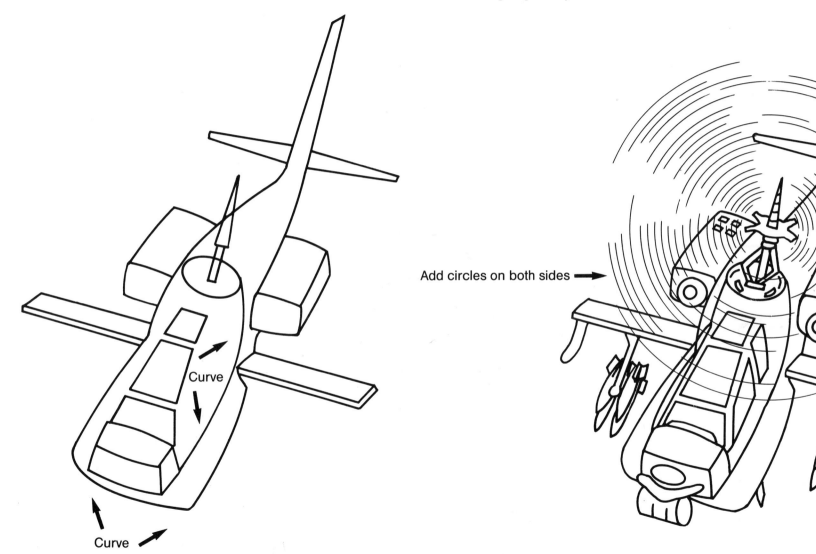

Curve

Curve

Add circles on both sides ➜

SOVIET MiG 29 FULCRUM

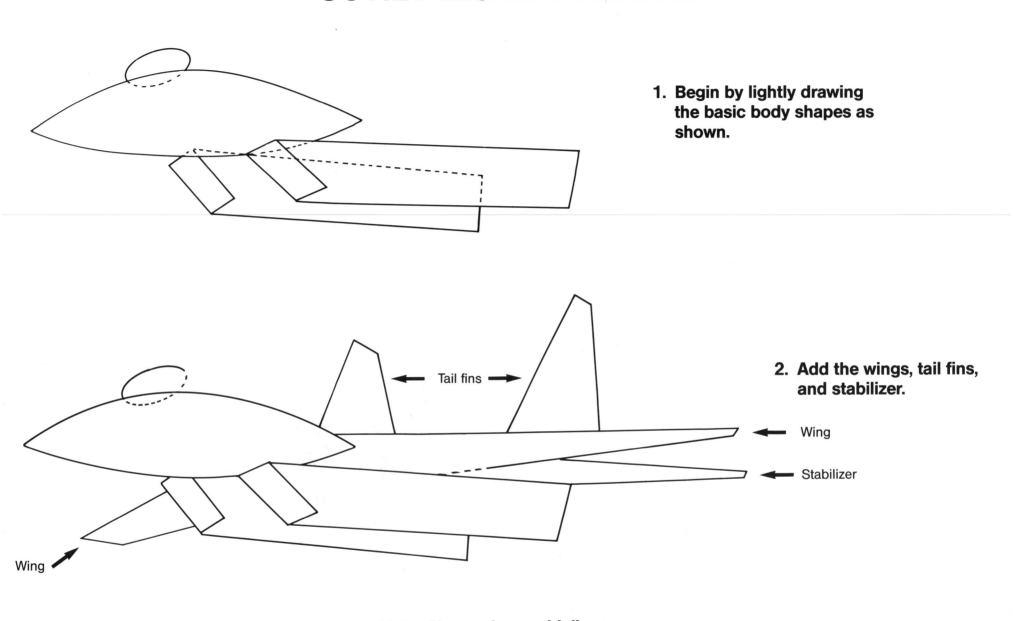

1. **Begin by lightly drawing the basic body shapes as shown.**

Tail fins

2. **Add the wings, tail fins, and stabilizer.**

Wing

Stabilizer

Wing

Note: Always draw guidelines lightly. If you don't like the way something looks, erase and try again.

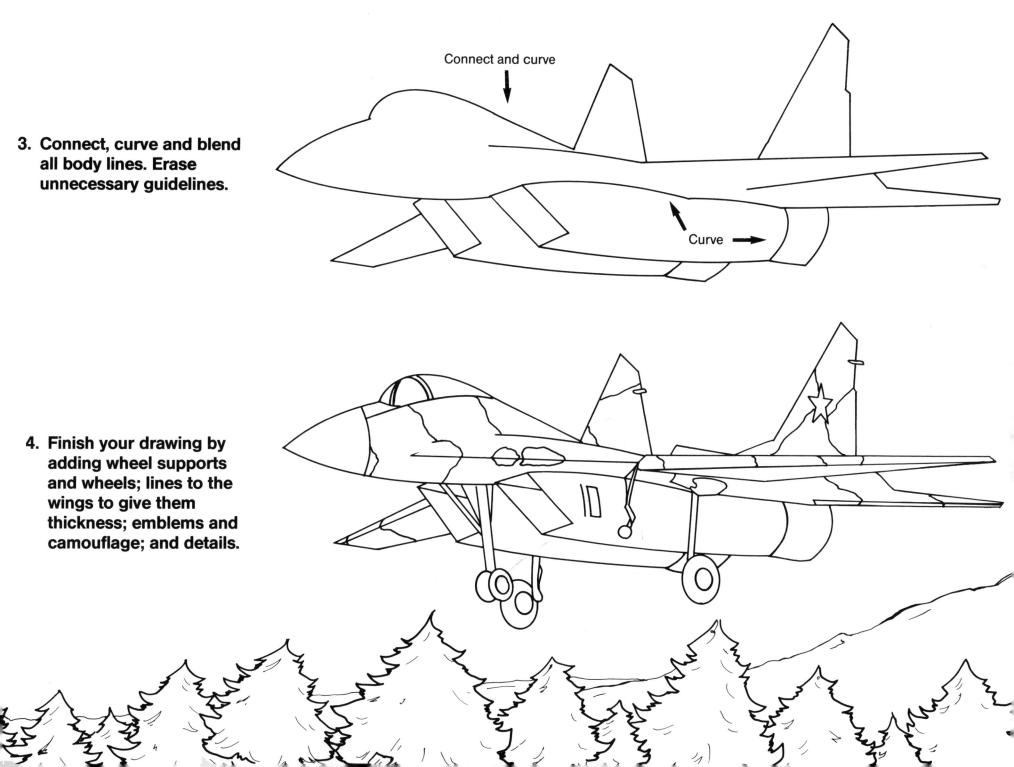

3. Connect, curve and blend all body lines. Erase unnecessary guidelines.

Connect and curve

Curve ➡

4. Finish your drawing by adding wheel supports and wheels; lines to the wings to give them thickness; emblems and camouflage; and details.

F-14 TOMCAT

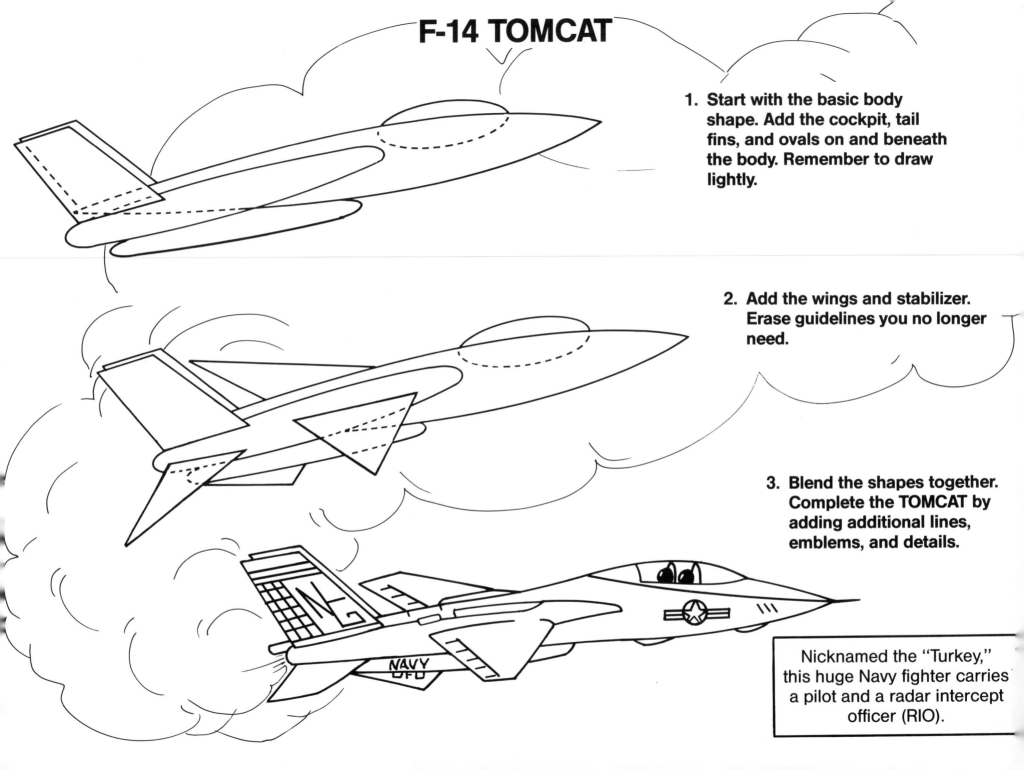

1. Start with the basic body shape. Add the cockpit, tail fins, and ovals on and beneath the body. Remember to draw lightly.

2. Add the wings and stabilizer. Erase guidelines you no longer need.

3. Blend the shapes together. Complete the TOMCAT by adding additional lines, emblems, and details.

Nicknamed the "Turkey," this huge Navy fighter carries a pilot and a radar intercept officer (RIO).

NAVY

HOW TO DRAW TRUCKS

Illustrated by
Karen Ann McKee

ANTIQUE TRUCK

1. Start your drawing by sketching simple rectangles for the body, and overlapping circles for the wheels.

Artist's Hint: Guideline shapes and lines should always be lightly drawn. They will be easier to erase later.

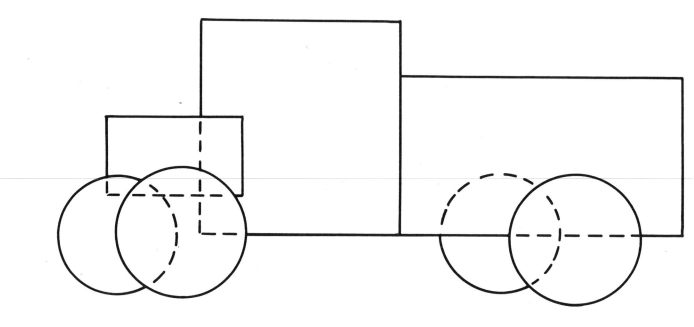

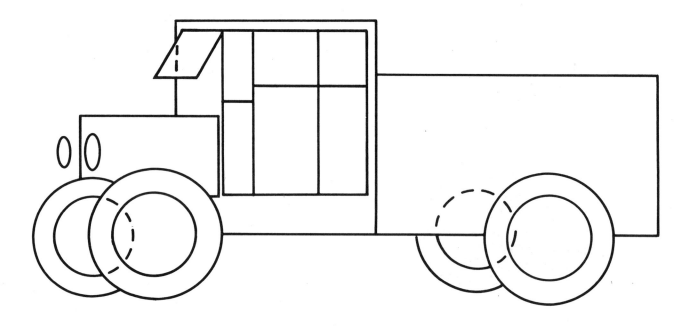

2. Add inner circles to form the tires. Then add oval headlights and additional lines for the door and windows.

3. Curve the hood and round the top. Draw the rounded front and rear fenders and complete the headlights. Erase any guidelines you no longer need.

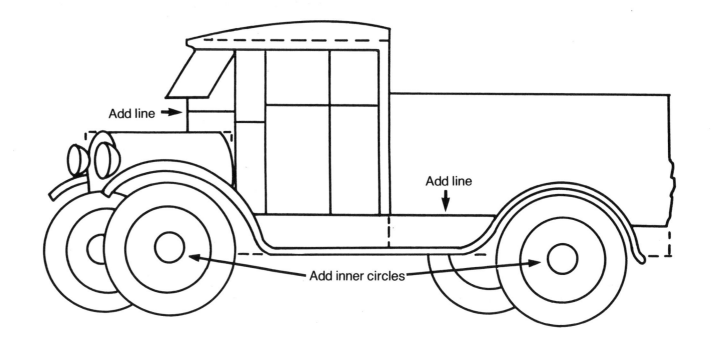

Add line →

Add line

Add inner circles

4. Add spokes to the wheels, and door and body lines. Finish your antique truck with shading and other details. What else do you think this truck could be hauling? Draw it.

APPLES   APPLES   APPLES

PICK-UP TRUCK

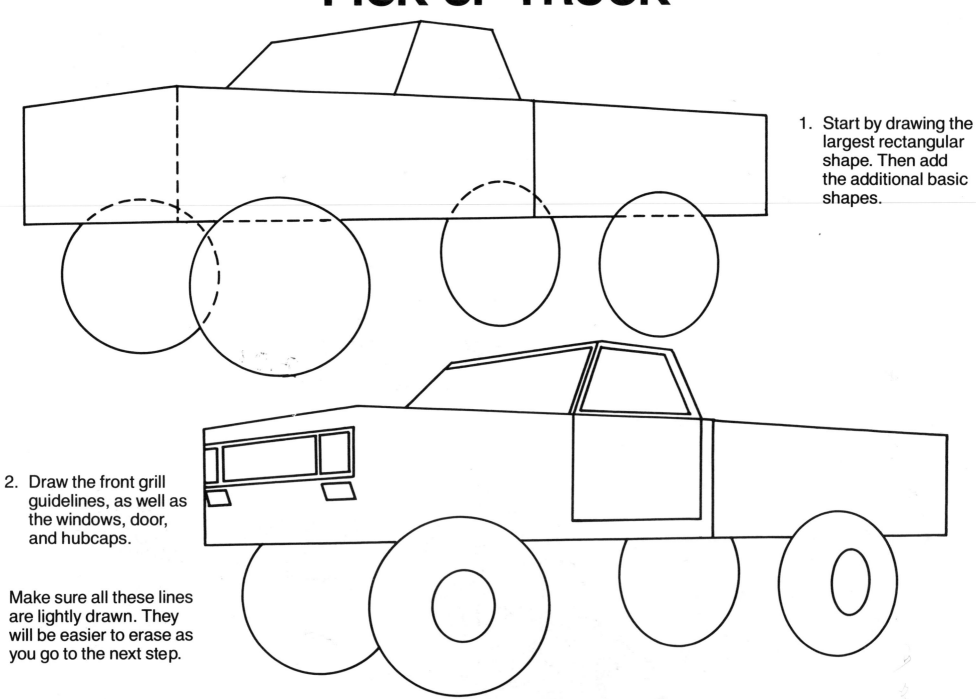

1. Start by drawing the largest rectangular shape. Then add the additional basic shapes.

2. Draw the front grill guidelines, as well as the windows, door, and hubcaps.

Make sure all these lines are lightly drawn. They will be easier to erase as you go to the next step.

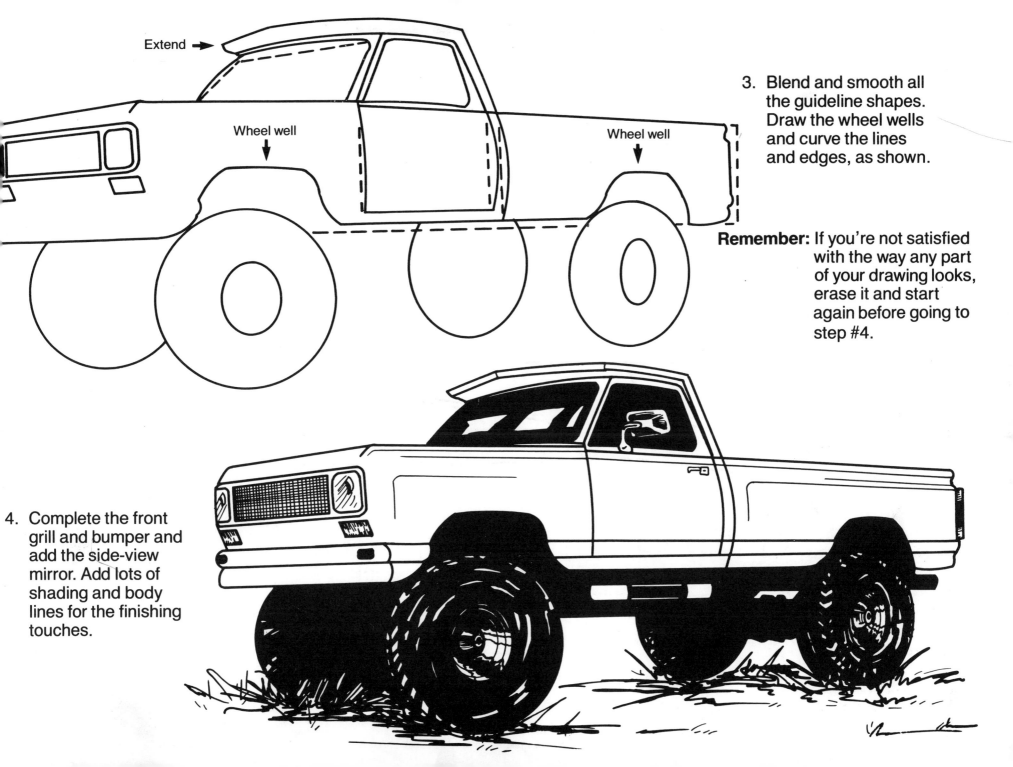

Extend →

Wheel well

Wheel well

3. Blend and smooth all the guideline shapes. Draw the wheel wells and curve the lines and edges, as shown.

Remember: If you're not satisfied with the way any part of your drawing looks, erase it and start again before going to step #4.

4. Complete the front grill and bumper and add the side-view mirror. Add lots of shading and body lines for the finishing touches.

AMBULANCE

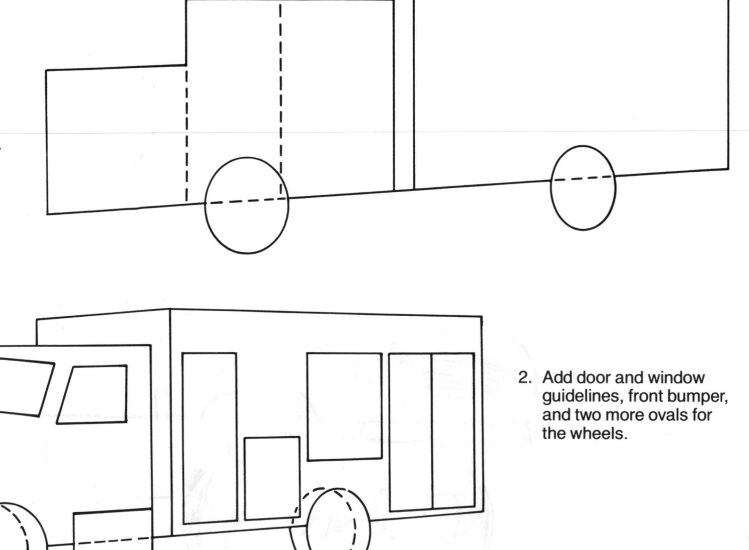

1. Begin by drawing four rectangular shapes and two small ovals.

Artist's Hint: It's often easier to begin by drawing the largest shape first.

2. Add door and window guidelines, front bumper, and two more ovals for the wheels.

Erase any unnecessary lines as you go along

Curve and shape the cab with rounded lines. Add the fender, wheel wells, and cab door. Complete the bumper.

Note: If you're not satisfied with the way your drawing looks, erase and start again. Practice makes perfect!

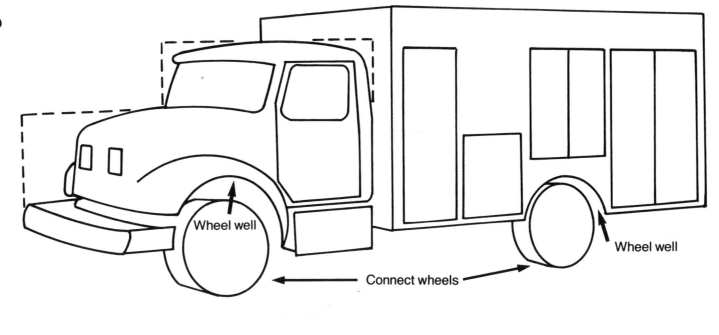

Wheel well

Wheel well

Connect wheels

4. Complete the ambulance by adding lots of details and shading. Note the two sirens and rear-view mirror. Now your ambulance is ready for an emergency.

OFF-ROAD 4 X 4

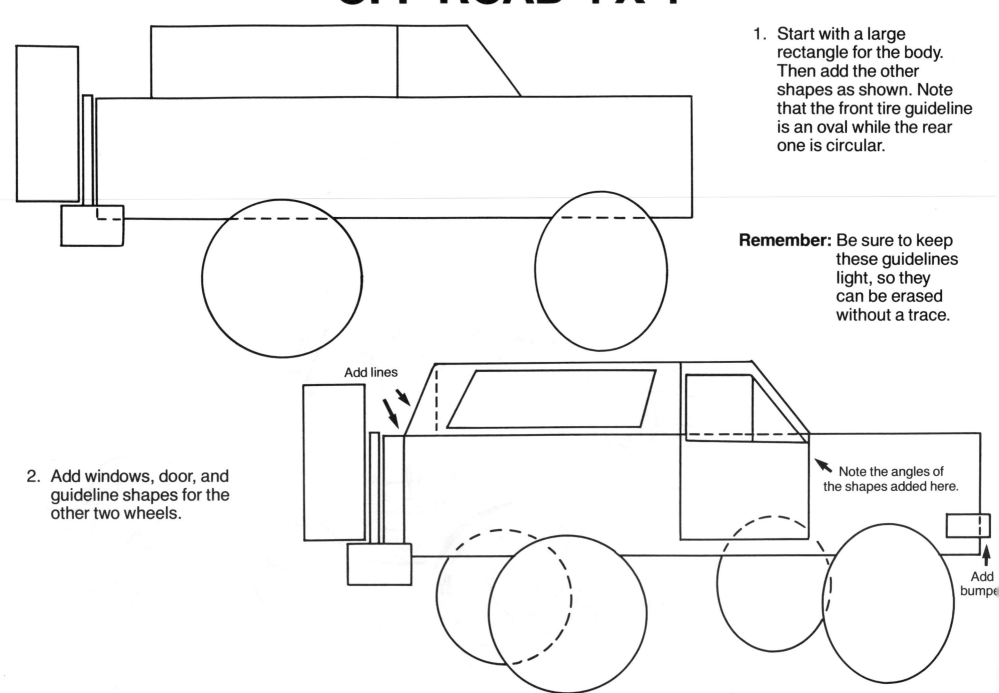

1. Start with a large rectangle for the body. Then add the other shapes as shown. Note that the front tire guideline is an oval while the rear one is circular.

Remember: Be sure to keep these guidelines light, so they can be erased without a trace.

Add lines

Note the angles of the shapes added here.

2. Add windows, door, and guideline shapes for the other two wheels.

Add bumpe

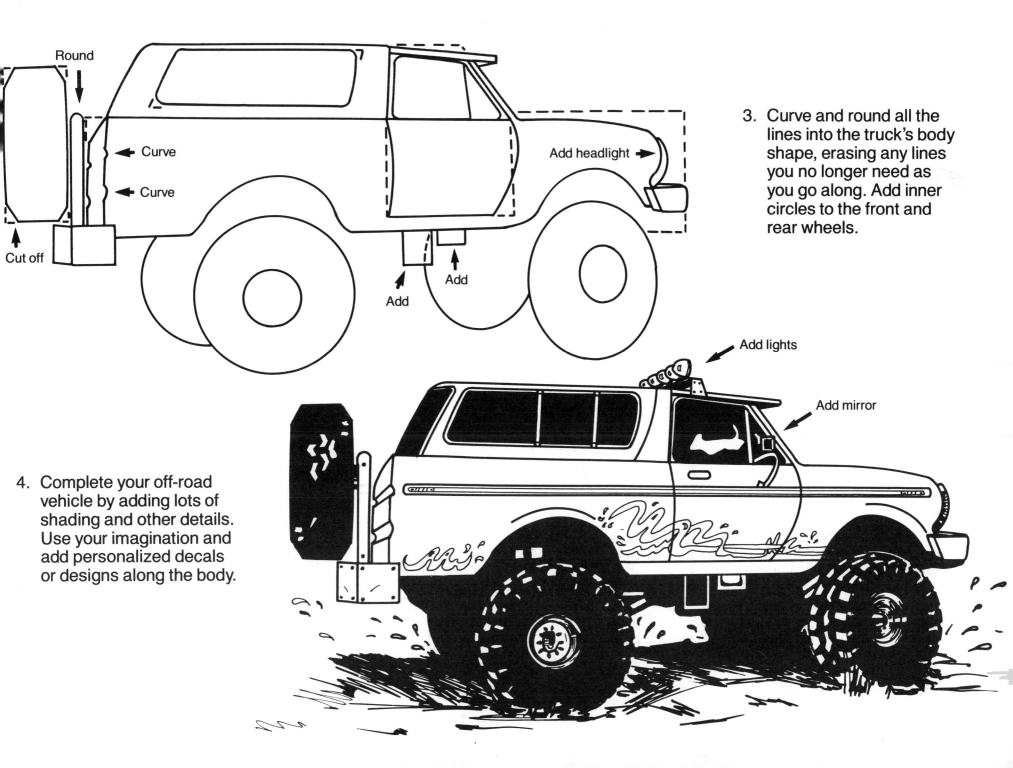

Round

Curve

Curve

Cut off

Add headlight

Add

Add

3. Curve and round all the lines into the truck's body shape, erasing any lines you no longer need as you go along. Add inner circles to the front and rear wheels.

Add lights

Add mirror

4. Complete your off-road vehicle by adding lots of shading and other details. Use your imagination and add personalized decals or designs along the body.

18 WHEELER

1. Start this giant truck by drawing three overlapping rectangles. Then add a long rectangular shape for the side of the trailer. Finish step #1 by drawing the bumper and six oval guidelines for the wheels.

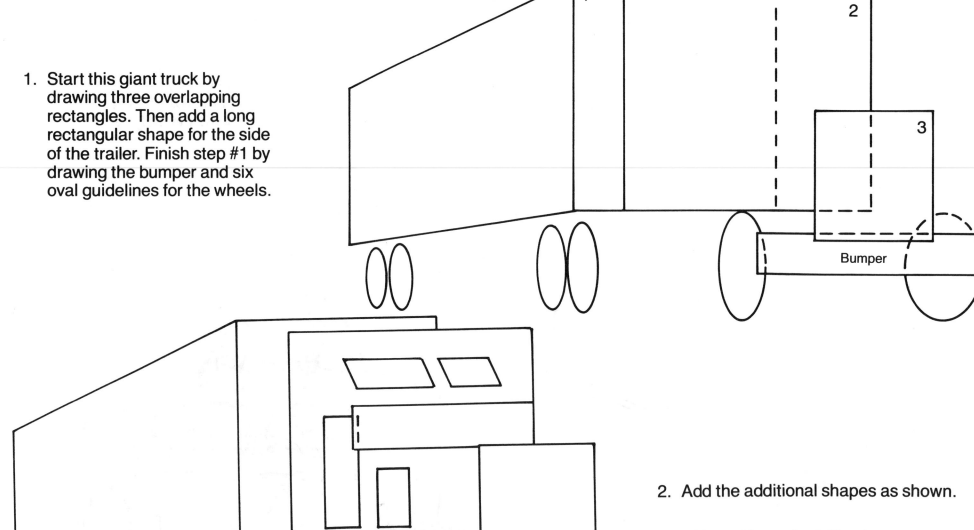

2. Add the additional shapes as shown.

Note: If you don't like the way any part of your drawing looks, erase it and start again.

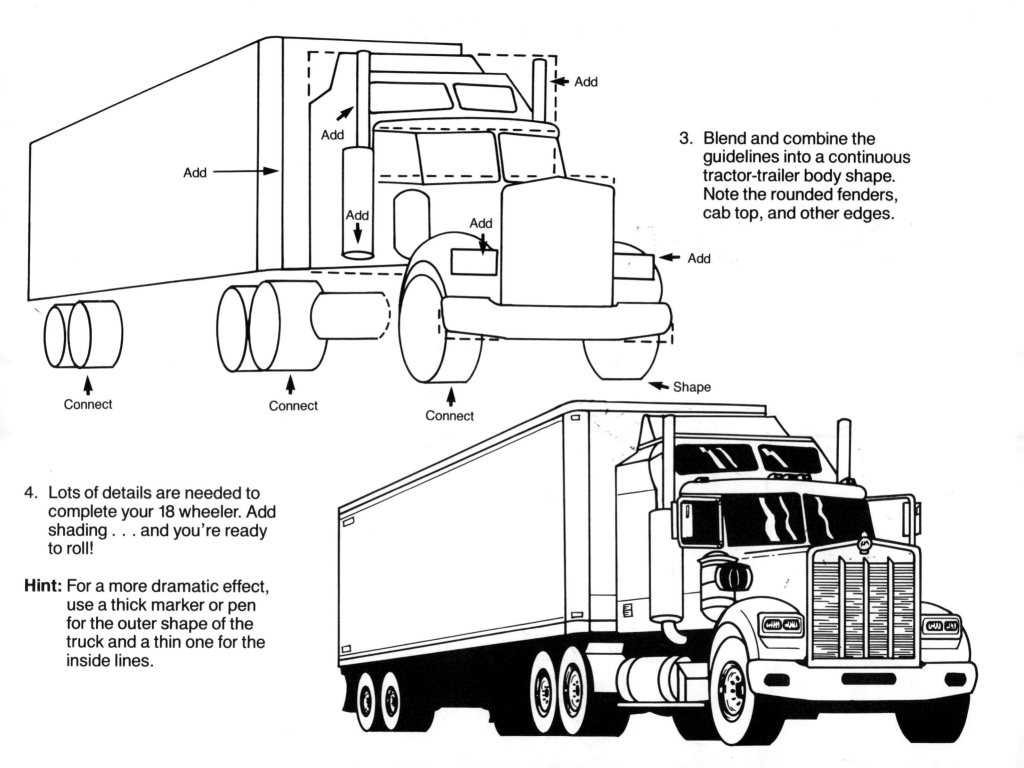

Add

Add

Add

Add

Add

Add

3. Blend and combine the guidelines into a continuous tractor-trailer body shape. Note the rounded fenders, cab top, and other edges.

Add

Connect

Connect

Connect

Shape

4. Lots of details are needed to complete your 18 wheeler. Add shading . . . and you're ready to roll!

Hint: For a more dramatic effect, use a thick marker or pen for the outer shape of the truck and a thin one for the inside lines.

MONSTER TRUCK

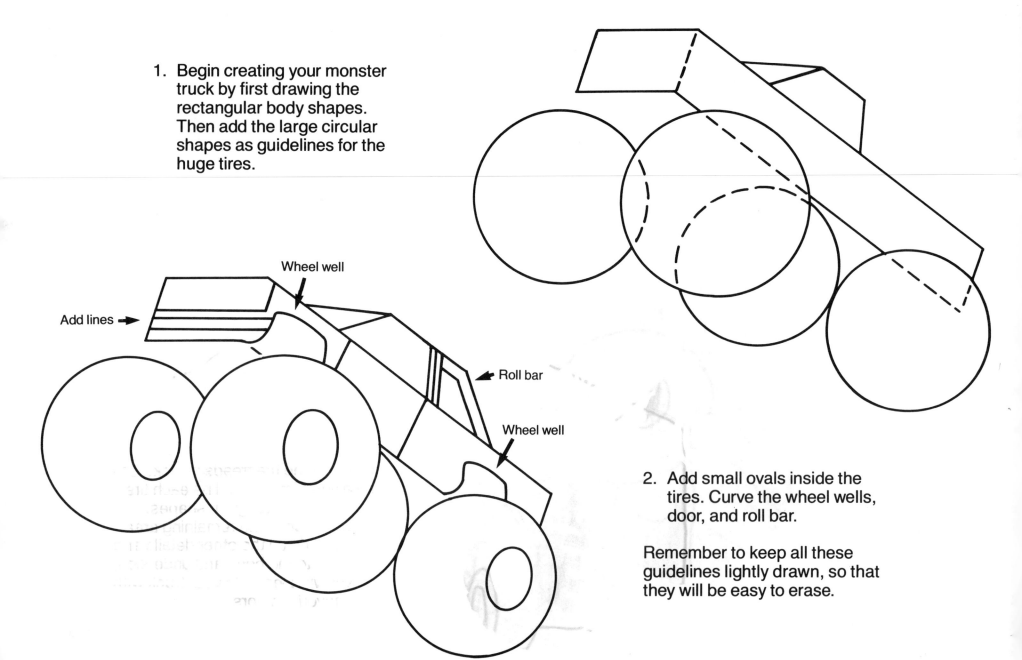

1. Begin creating your monster truck by first drawing the rectangular body shapes. Then add the large circular shapes as guidelines for the huge tires.

Wheel well

Add lines →

← Roll bar

Wheel well

2. Add small ovals inside the tires. Curve the wheel wells, door, and roll bar.

Remember to keep all these guidelines lightly drawn, so that they will be easy to erase.

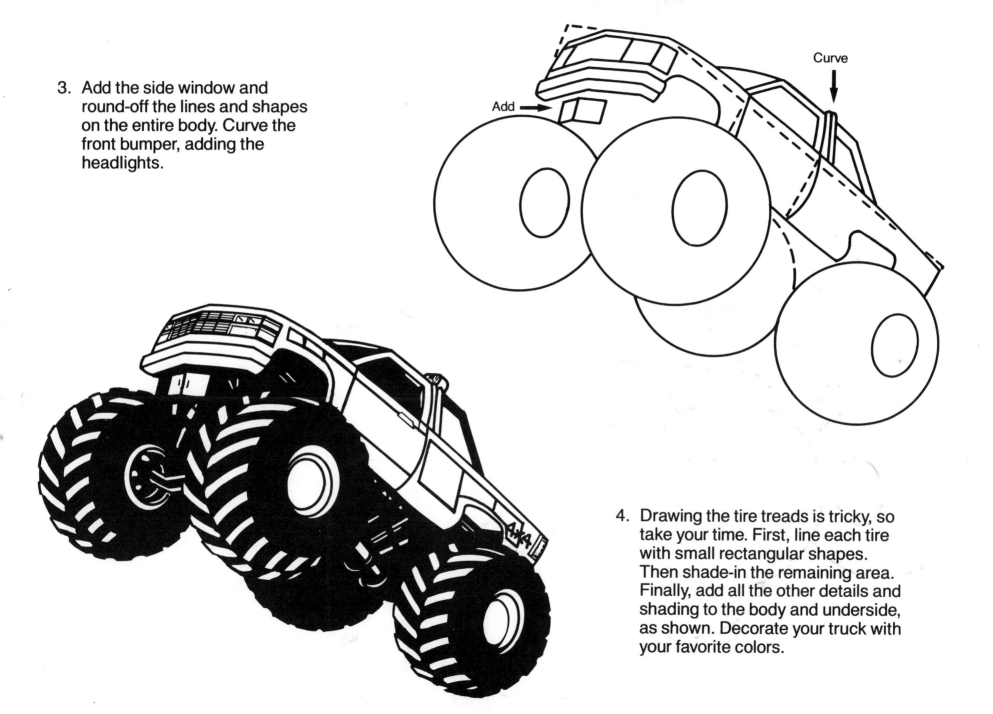

3. Add the side window and round-off the lines and shapes on the entire body. Curve the front bumper, adding the headlights.

Curve

Add

4. Drawing the tire treads is tricky, so take your time. First, line each tire with small rectangular shapes. Then shade-in the remaining area. Finally, add all the other details and shading to the body and underside, as shown. Decorate your truck with your favorite colors.

ICE-CREAM TRUCK

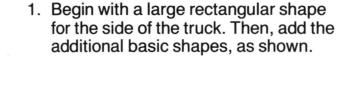

1. Begin with a large rectangular shape for the side of the truck. Then, add the additional basic shapes, as shown.

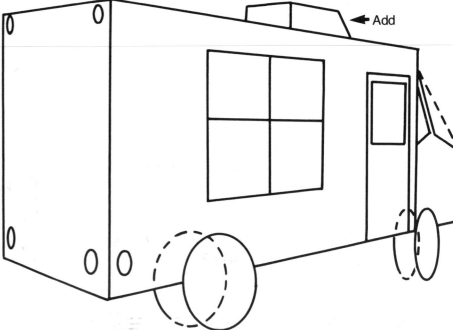

← Add

2. Add taillights, windows, and additional ovals for the wheels. Start erasing any guidelines you no longer need.

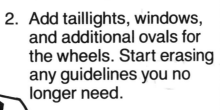

3. Complete the overall shape of the ice-cream truck. (Details and shading always come last.) Note the rounded edges and wheel wells. Draw your ice cream favorites on the sides of the truck. Then listen carefully for the ringing bells.

SANITATION TRUCK

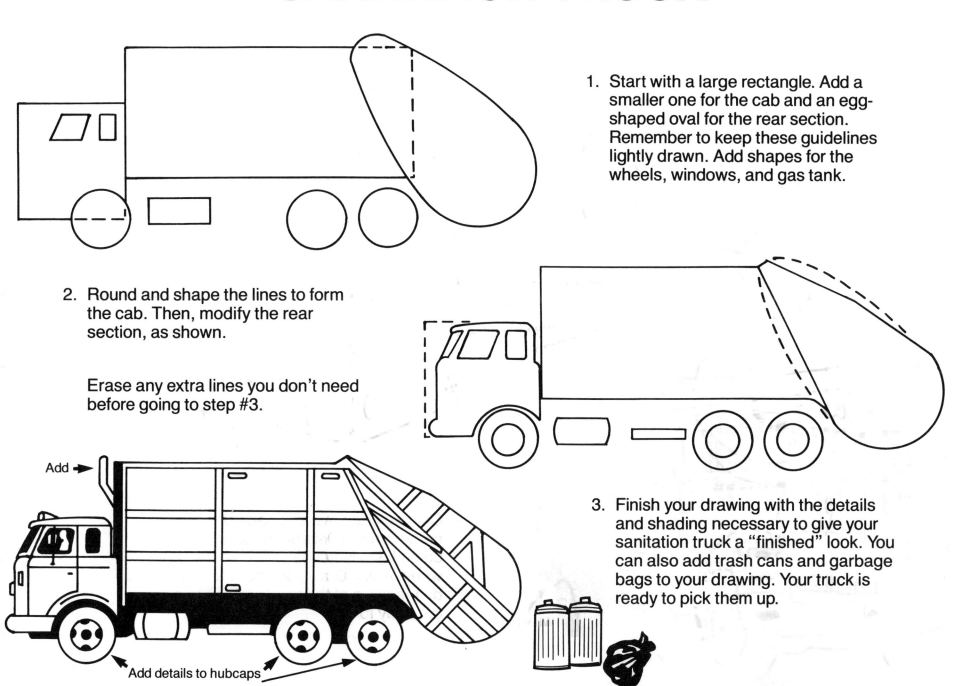

1. Start with a large rectangle. Add a smaller one for the cab and an egg-shaped oval for the rear section. Remember to keep these guidelines lightly drawn. Add shapes for the wheels, windows, and gas tank.

2. Round and shape the lines to form the cab. Then, modify the rear section, as shown.

   Erase any extra lines you don't need before going to step #3.

3. Finish your drawing with the details and shading necessary to give your sanitation truck a "finished" look. You can also add trash cans and garbage bags to your drawing. Your truck is ready to pick them up.

Add ➤

Add details to hubcaps

DUMP TRUCK

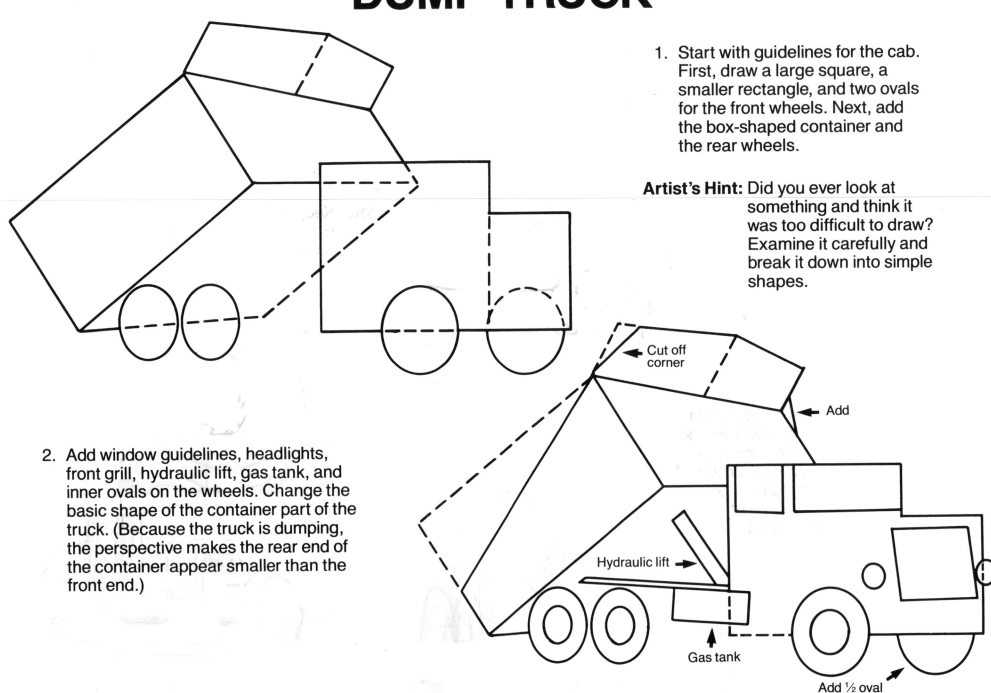

1. Start with guidelines for the cab. First, draw a large square, a smaller rectangle, and two ovals for the front wheels. Next, add the box-shaped container and the rear wheels.

Artist's Hint: Did you ever look at something and think it was too difficult to draw? Examine it carefully and break it down into simple shapes.

2. Add window guidelines, headlights, front grill, hydraulic lift, gas tank, and inner ovals on the wheels. Change the basic shape of the container part of the truck. (Because the truck is dumping, the perspective makes the rear end of the container appear smaller than the front end.)

Cut off corner

Add

Hydraulic lift

Gas tank

Add ½ oval

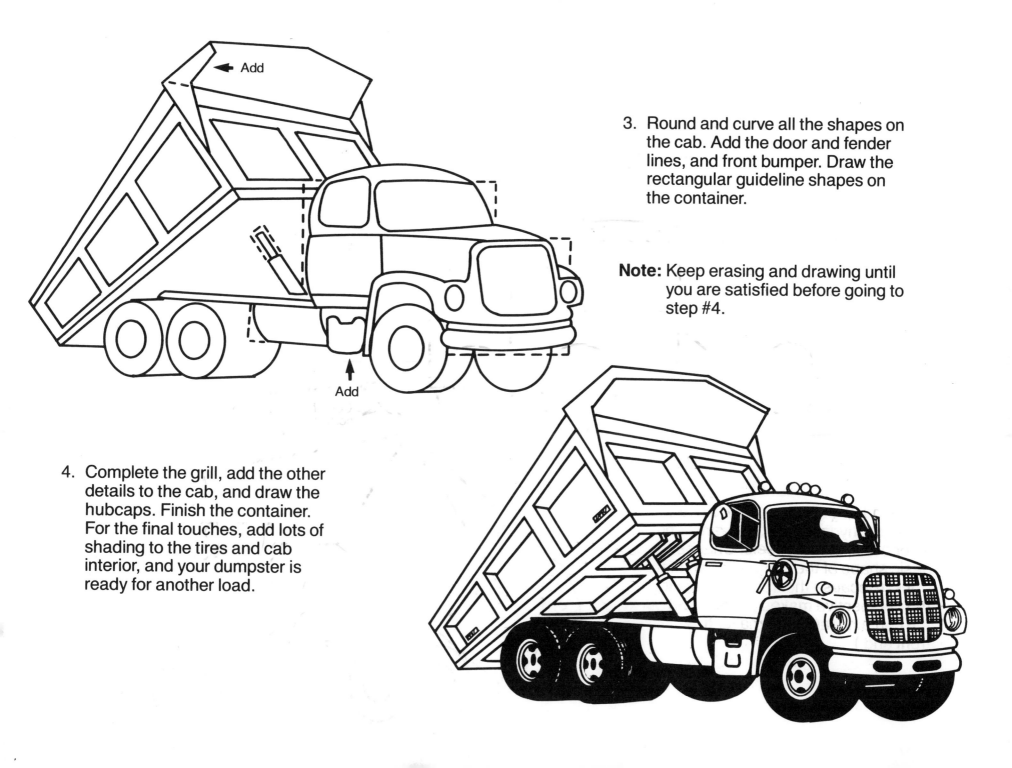

Add

3. Round and curve all the shapes on the cab. Add the door and fender lines, and front bumper. Draw the rectangular guideline shapes on the container.

Note: Keep erasing and drawing until you are satisfied before going to step #4.

Add

4. Complete the grill, add the other details to the cab, and draw the hubcaps. Finish the container. For the final touches, add lots of shading to the tires and cab interior, and your dumpster is ready for another load.

CUSTOMIZED 4 X 4

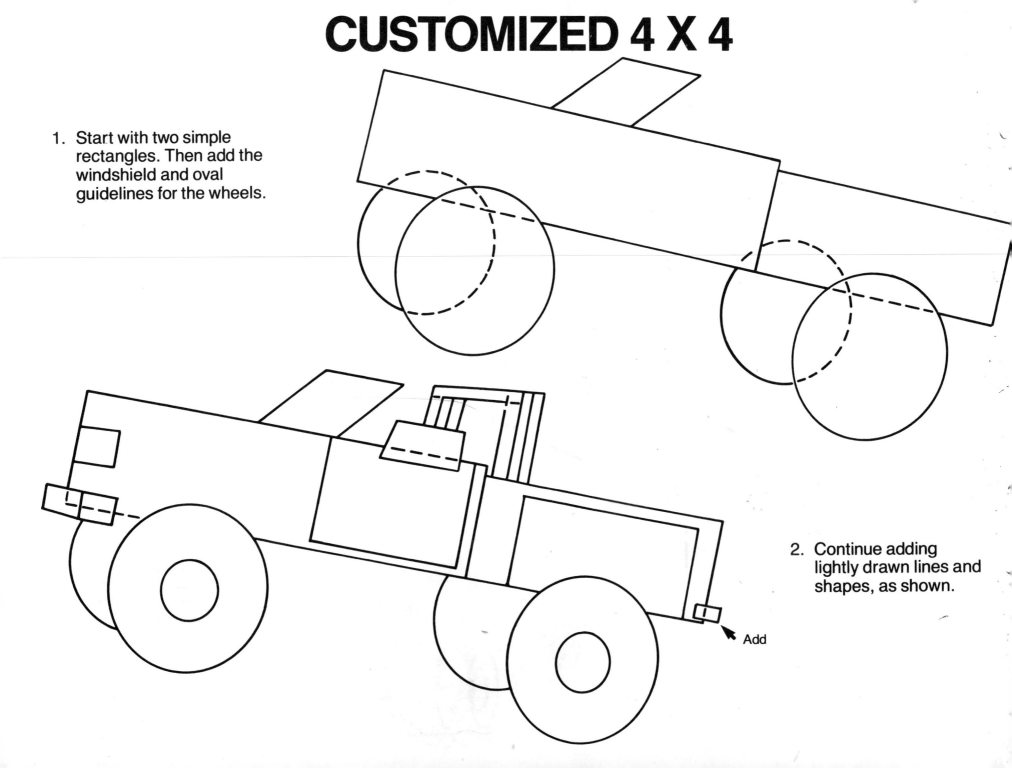

1. Start with two simple rectangles. Then add the windshield and oval guidelines for the wheels.

2. Continue adding lightly drawn lines and shapes, as shown.

Add

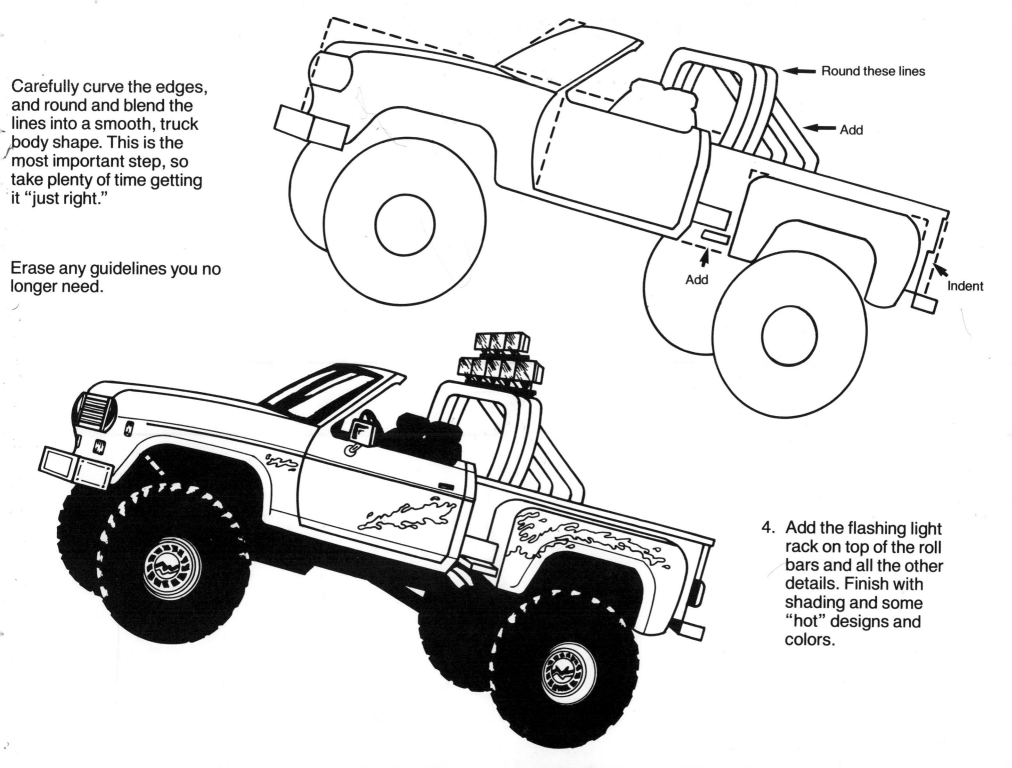

Carefully curve the edges, and round and blend the lines into a smooth, truck body shape. This is the most important step, so take plenty of time getting it "just right."

Erase any guidelines you no longer need.

Round these lines

Add

Add

Indent

4. Add the flashing light rack on top of the roll bars and all the other details. Finish with shading and some "hot" designs and colors.

DELIVERY TRUCK

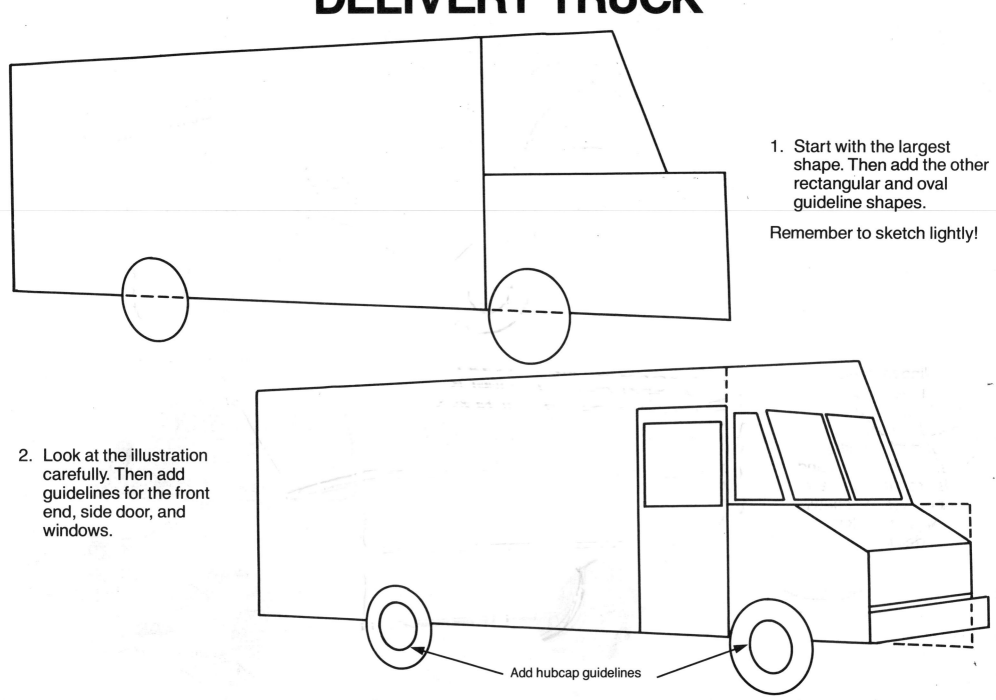

1. Start with the largest shape. Then add the other rectangular and oval guideline shapes.

   Remember to sketch lightly!

2. Look at the illustration carefully. Then add guidelines for the front end, side door, and windows.

Add hubcap guidelines

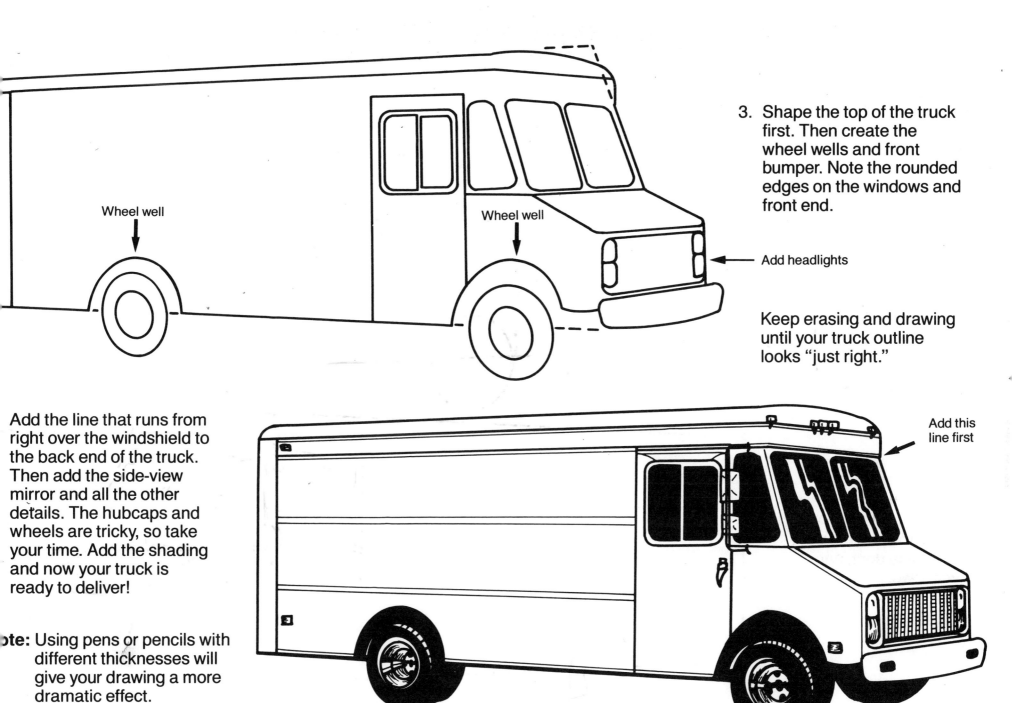

Wheel well

Wheel well

3. Shape the top of the truck first. Then create the wheel wells and front bumper. Note the rounded edges on the windows and front end.

Add headlights

Keep erasing and drawing until your truck outline looks "just right."

Add this line first

Add the line that runs from right over the windshield to the back end of the truck. Then add the side-view mirror and all the other details. The hubcaps and wheels are tricky, so take your time. Add the shading and now your truck is ready to deliver!

ote: Using pens or pencils with different thicknesses will give your drawing a more dramatic effect.

TOW TRUCK

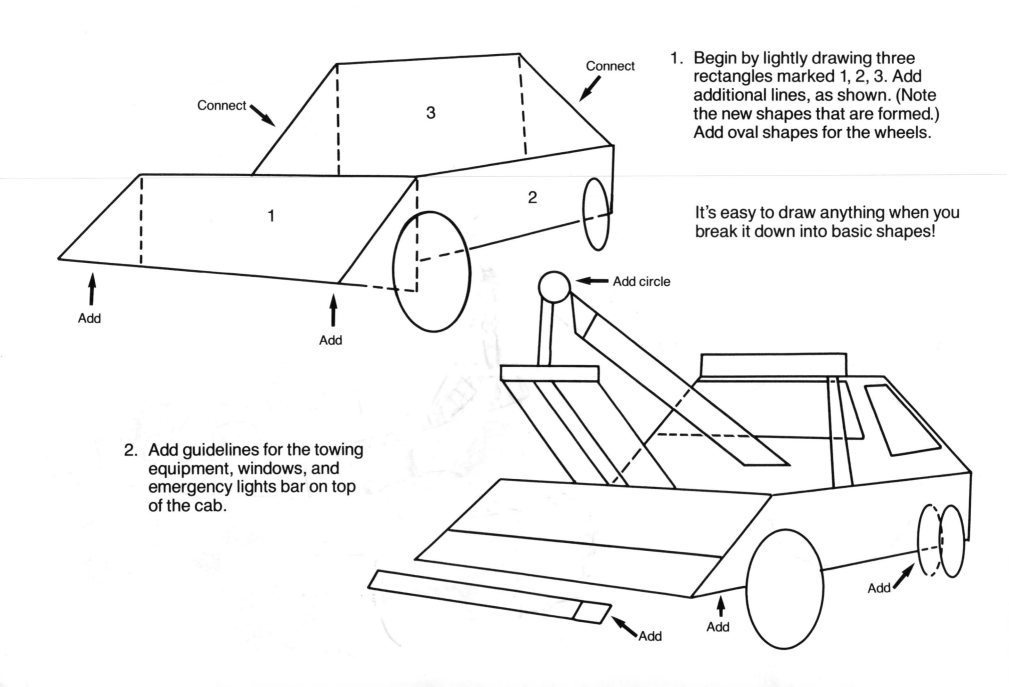

Connect

Connect

Add

Add

3

1

2

Add circle

1. Begin by lightly drawing three rectangles marked 1, 2, 3. Add additional lines, as shown. (Note the new shapes that are formed.) Add oval shapes for the wheels.

It's easy to draw anything when you break it down into basic shapes!

2. Add guidelines for the towing equipment, windows, and emergency lights bar on top of the cab.

Add

Add

Add

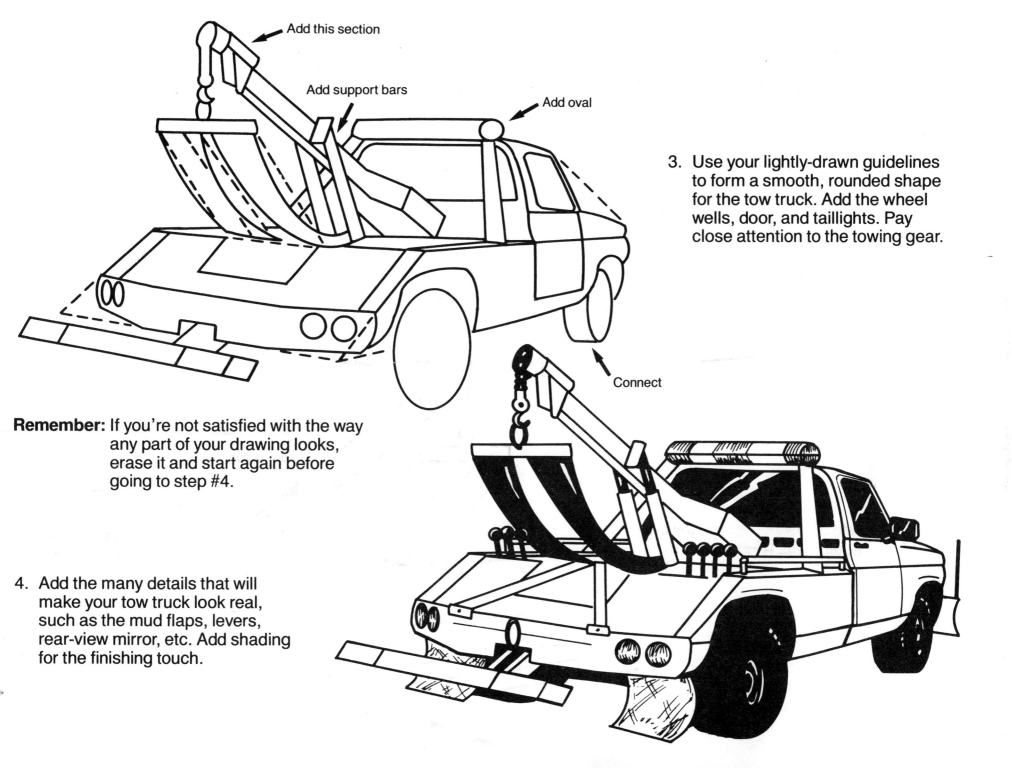

Add this section

Add support bars

Add oval

3. Use your lightly-drawn guidelines to form a smooth, rounded shape for the tow truck. Add the wheel wells, door, and taillights. Pay close attention to the towing gear.

Connect

Remember: If you're not satisfied with the way any part of your drawing looks, erase it and start again before going to step #4.

4. Add the many details that will make your tow truck look real, such as the mud flaps, levers, rear-view mirror, etc. Add shading for the finishing touch.

FIRE ENGINE

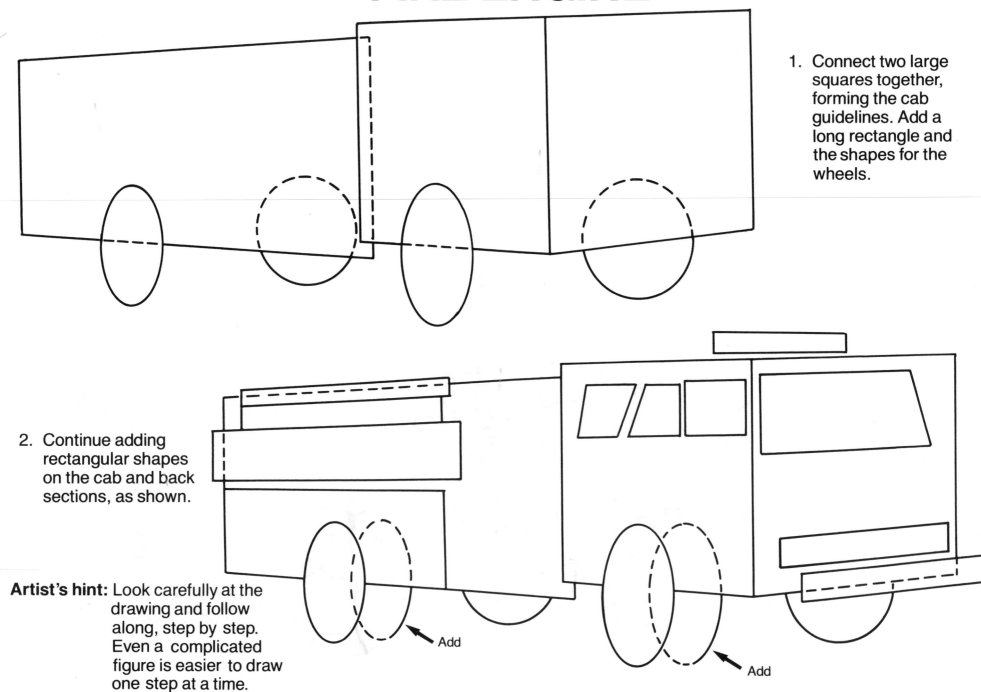

1. Connect two large squares together, forming the cab guidelines. Add a long rectangle and the shapes for the wheels.

2. Continue adding rectangular shapes on the cab and back sections, as shown.

Artist's hint: Look carefully at the drawing and follow along, step by step. Even a complicated figure is easier to draw one step at a time.

Add

Add

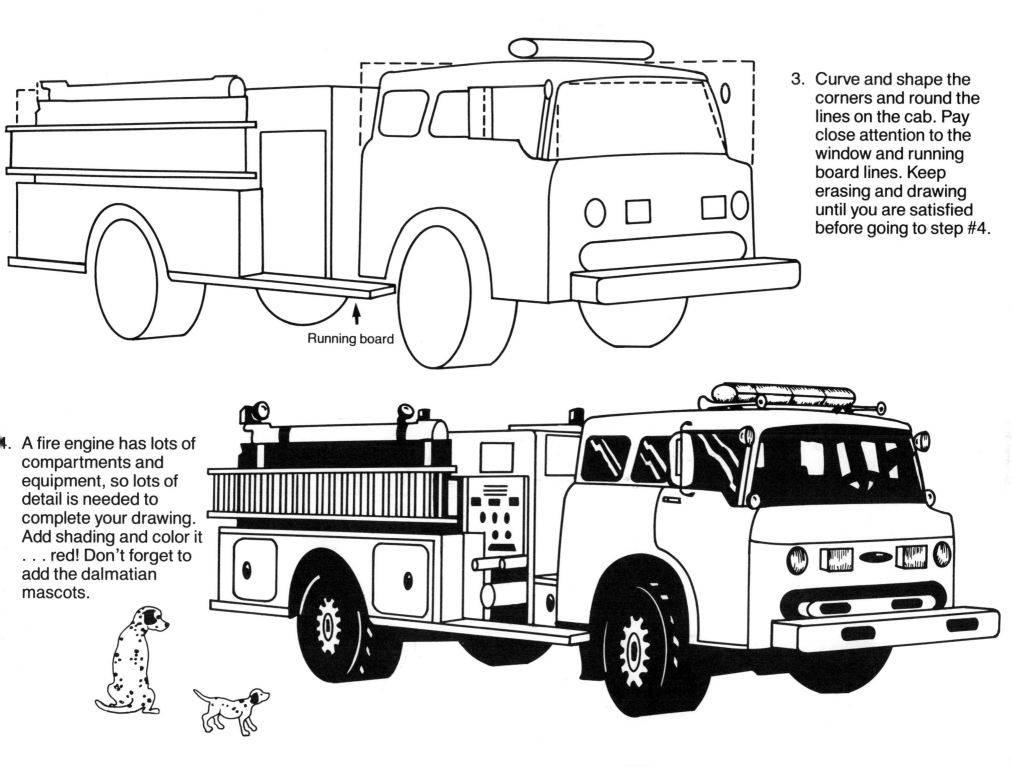

3. Curve and shape the corners and round the lines on the cab. Pay close attention to the window and running board lines. Keep erasing and drawing until you are satisfied before going to step #4.

Running board

4. A fire engine has lots of compartments and equipment, so lots of detail is needed to complete your drawing. Add shading and color it . . . red! Don't forget to add the dalmatian mascots.

CEMENT MIXER

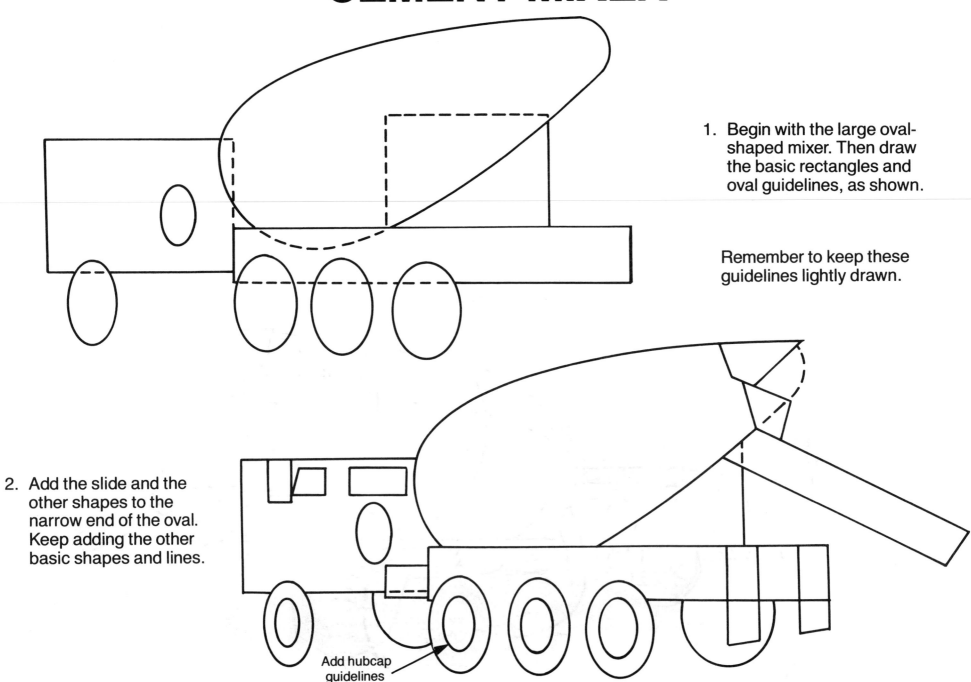

1. Begin with the large oval-shaped mixer. Then draw the basic rectangles and oval guidelines, as shown.

   Remember to keep these guidelines lightly drawn.

2. Add the slide and the other shapes to the narrow end of the oval. Keep adding the other basic shapes and lines.

Add hubcap guidelines

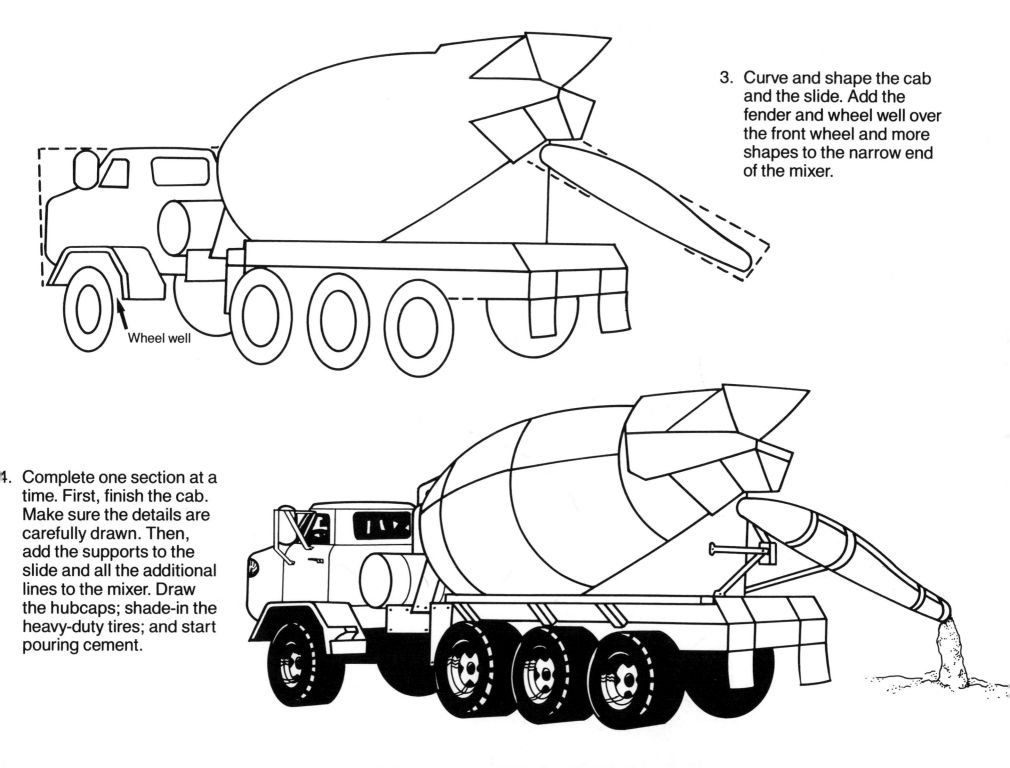

3. Curve and shape the cab and the slide. Add the fender and wheel well over the front wheel and more shapes to the narrow end of the mixer.

Wheel well

4. Complete one section at a time. First, finish the cab. Make sure the details are carefully drawn. Then, add the supports to the slide and all the additional lines to the mixer. Draw the hubcaps; shade-in the heavy-duty tires; and start pouring cement.

MINI PICK-UP TRUCK

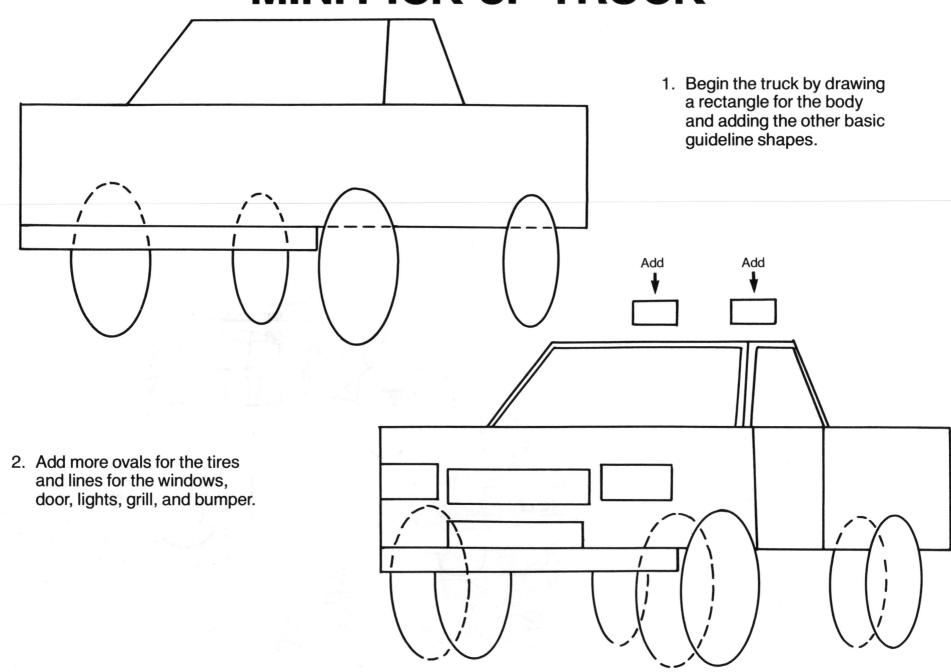

1. Begin the truck by drawing a rectangle for the body and adding the other basic guideline shapes.

Add

Add

2. Add more ovals for the tires and lines for the windows, door, lights, grill, and bumper.

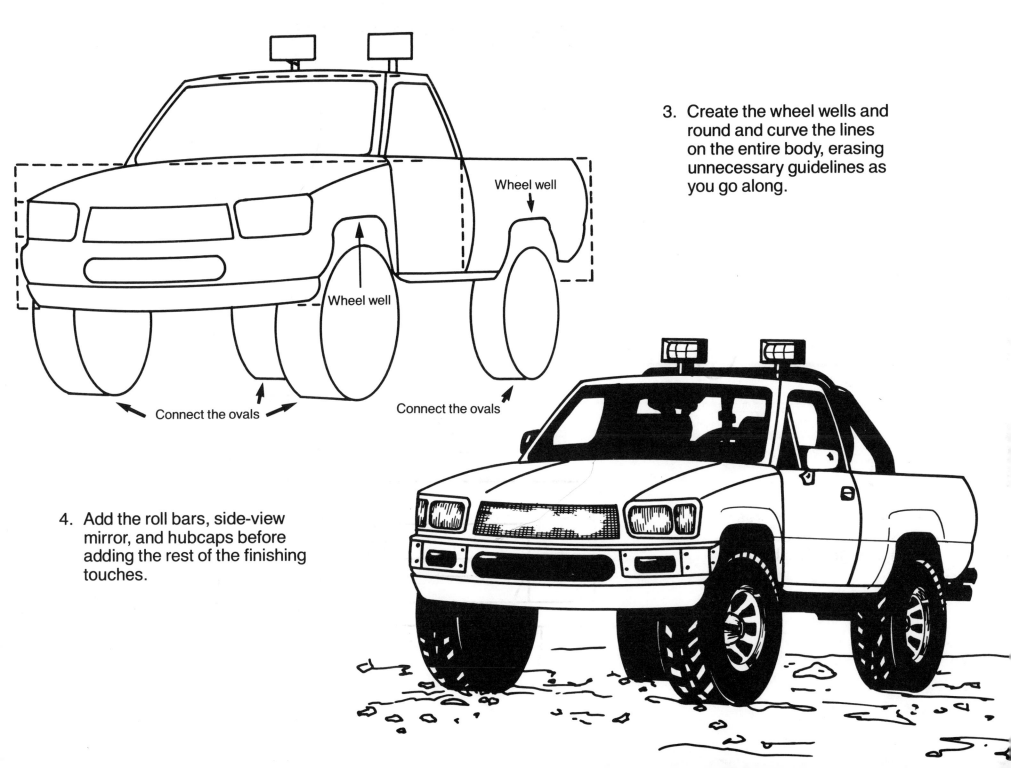

Wheel well

Wheel well

Connect the ovals   Connect the ovals

3. Create the wheel wells and round and curve the lines on the entire body, erasing unnecessary guidelines as you go along.

4. Add the roll bars, side-view mirror, and hubcaps before adding the rest of the finishing touches.

TANKER

1. Start with two circles—drawn far apart—and connec them with two straight lines. Then draw the additional basic shapes.

2. Add more basic shapes to the underside of the tank and to the cab

Add circles in each wheel

Add circles in each wheel

3. Curve the lines around the cab, adding details and erasing unnecessary lines as you go along. Complete the whee wells, hubcaps, and add all the shading.

What do you think the tanker is carrying?

HOW TO DRAW THINGS THAT FLY

Illustrated by
Georgene Griffen

HOT AIR BALLOON

A hot air balloon has no engine. It's powered by a propane gas burner that heats the air inside the balloon, causing it to rise.

1. Begin your drawing with a very large oval. Add simple shapes for the bottom of the balloon and for the basket that holds the passengers.

2. Draw curved lines on the balloon from the top to the bottom. Then complete the basket. The propane tank goes just above the passengers' heads.

3. The best part of drawing hot air balloons is the decorating. They come in all designs and colors. Decorate your balloon with your own design and add your favorite colors.

HANG GLIDER

A hang glider is powered only by the wind.
The pilot's body is used to steer and control the craft.

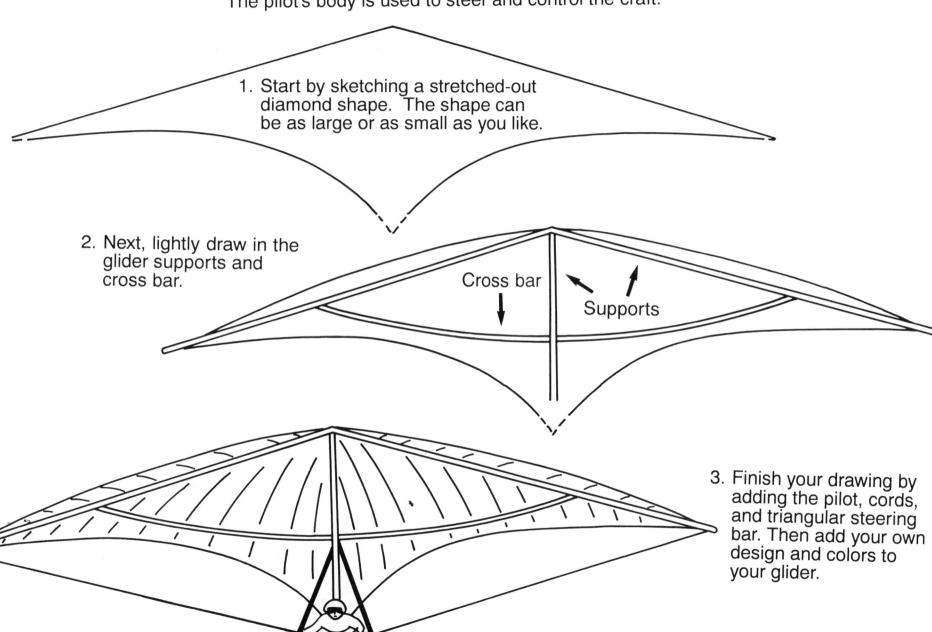

1. Start by sketching a stretched-out diamond shape. The shape can be as large or as small as you like.

2. Next, lightly draw in the glider supports and cross bar.

Cross bar

Supports

3. Finish your drawing by adding the pilot, cords, and triangular steering bar. Then add your own design and colors to your glider.

NORTHROP P-61B BLACK WIDOW

Introduced in 1944, the P-61B was the first airplane designed
expressly for night fighting.

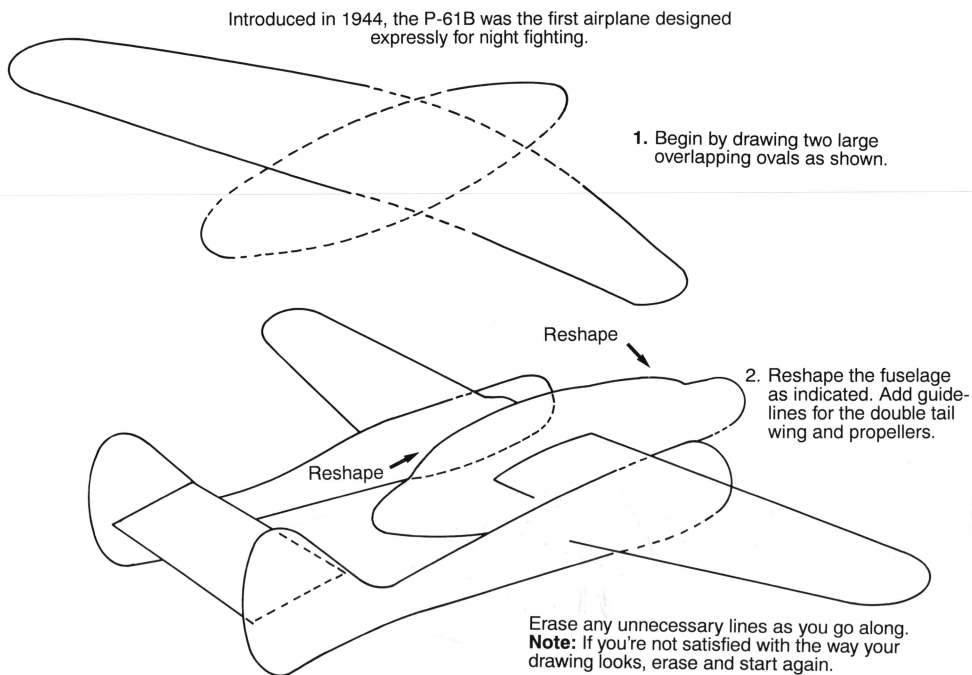

1. Begin by drawing two large
overlapping ovals as shown.

Reshape

2. Reshape the fuselage
as indicated. Add guide-
lines for the double tail
wing and propellers.

Reshape

Erase any unnecessary lines as you go along.
Note: If you're not satisfied with the way your
drawing looks, erase and start again.

Artist's Hint: It's often easier to begin by drawing the largest shape first.

3. Curve and shape the body and wing lines. Then add propellers and wheel.

4. Add the cockpit, rear windows, and lots of details. Take your time. The final steps will give your drawing a "finished" look.

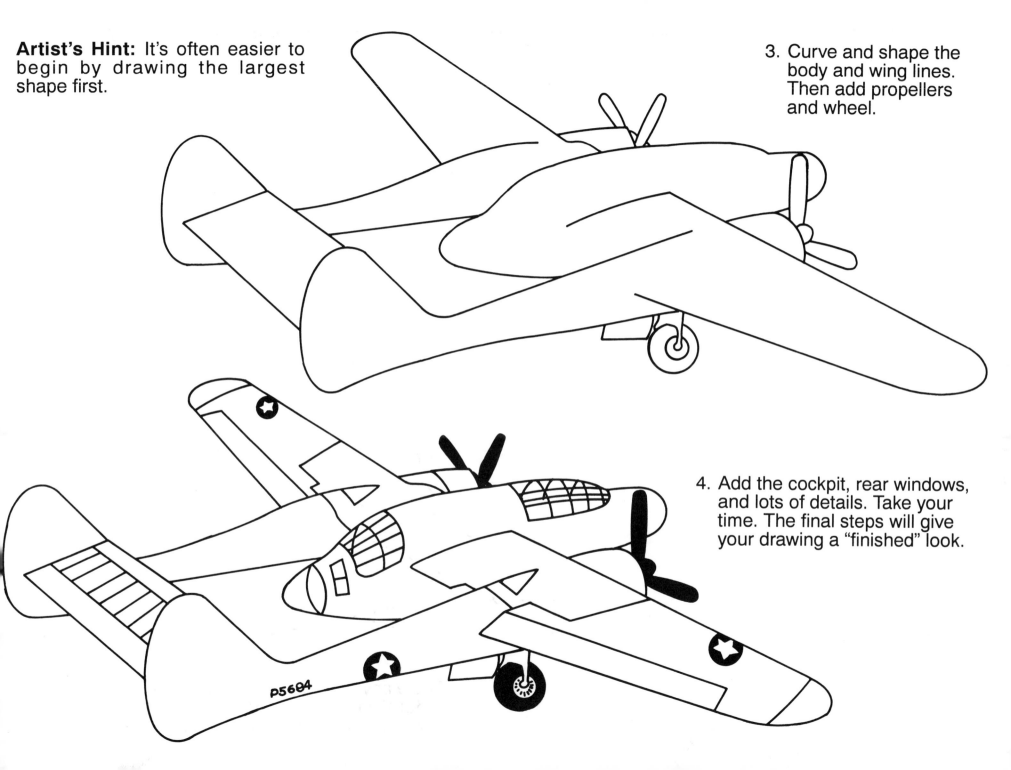

SOPWITH F-1 CAMEL

World War I British aircraft

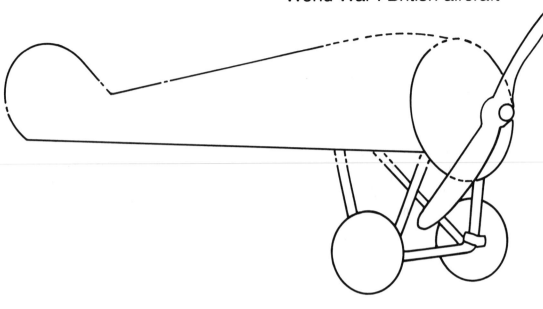

1. Start with the basic shapes for the fuselage. Then sketch in the propeller, engine, wheel supports, and wheels.

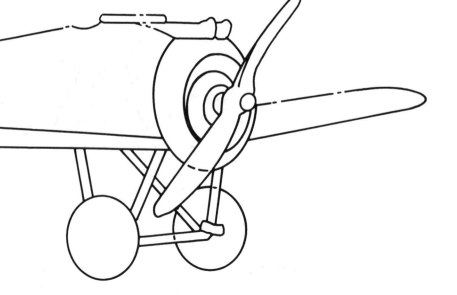

2. Add two large wings, one beneath the fuselage and one above. Draw the cockpit, guns, and rear stabilizer. Add more detail to the engine.

Start erasing any guidelines you no longer need.

Remember: Be sure to keep these guidelines light, so they can be erased without a trace.

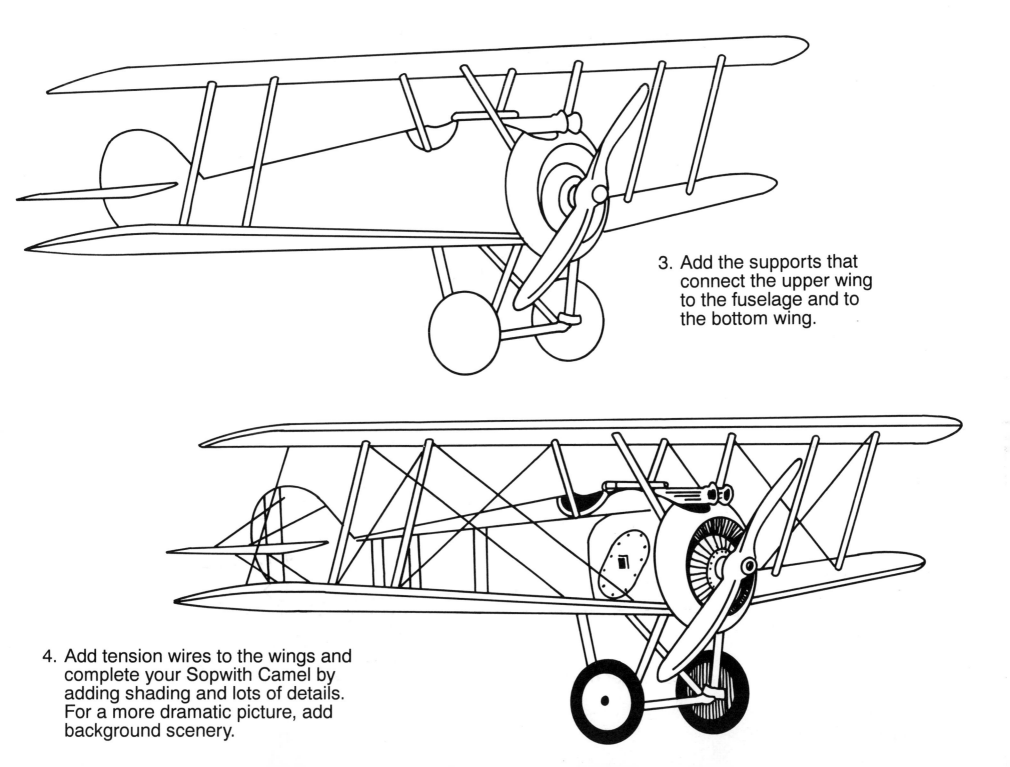

3. Add the supports that connect the upper wing to the fuselage and to the bottom wing.

4. Add tension wires to the wings and complete your Sopwith Camel by adding shading and lots of details. For a more dramatic picture, add background scenery.

AURORA HYPERSONIC SPY PLANE

Due to its top-secret nature, information on this airplane is incomplete.

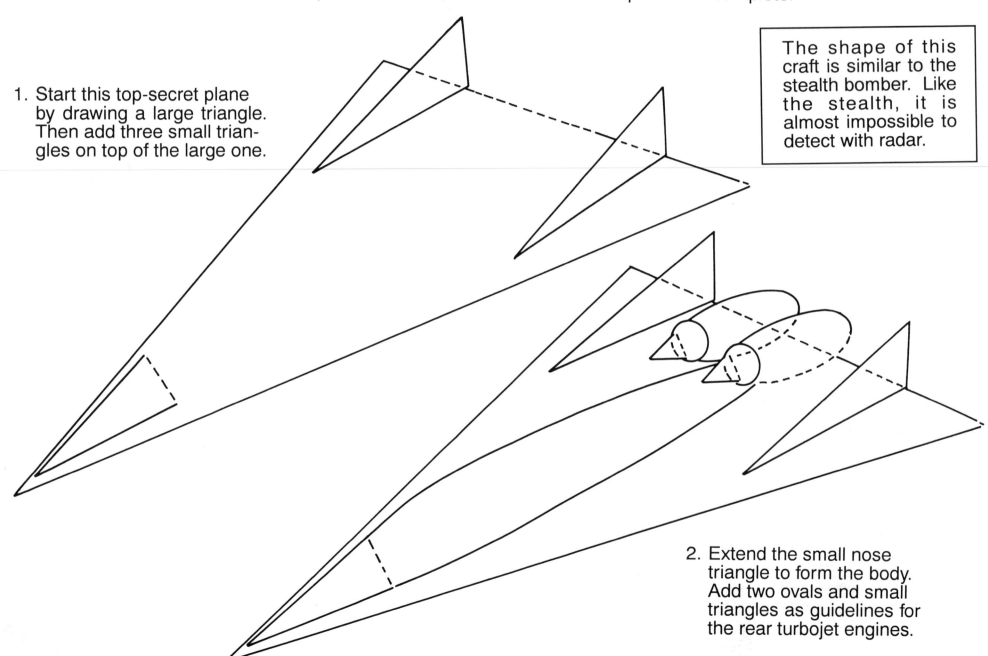

1. Start this top-secret plane by drawing a large triangle. Then add three small triangles on top of the large one.

The shape of this craft is similar to the stealth bomber. Like the stealth, it is almost impossible to detect with radar.

2. Extend the small nose triangle to form the body. Add two ovals and small triangles as guidelines for the rear turbojet engines.

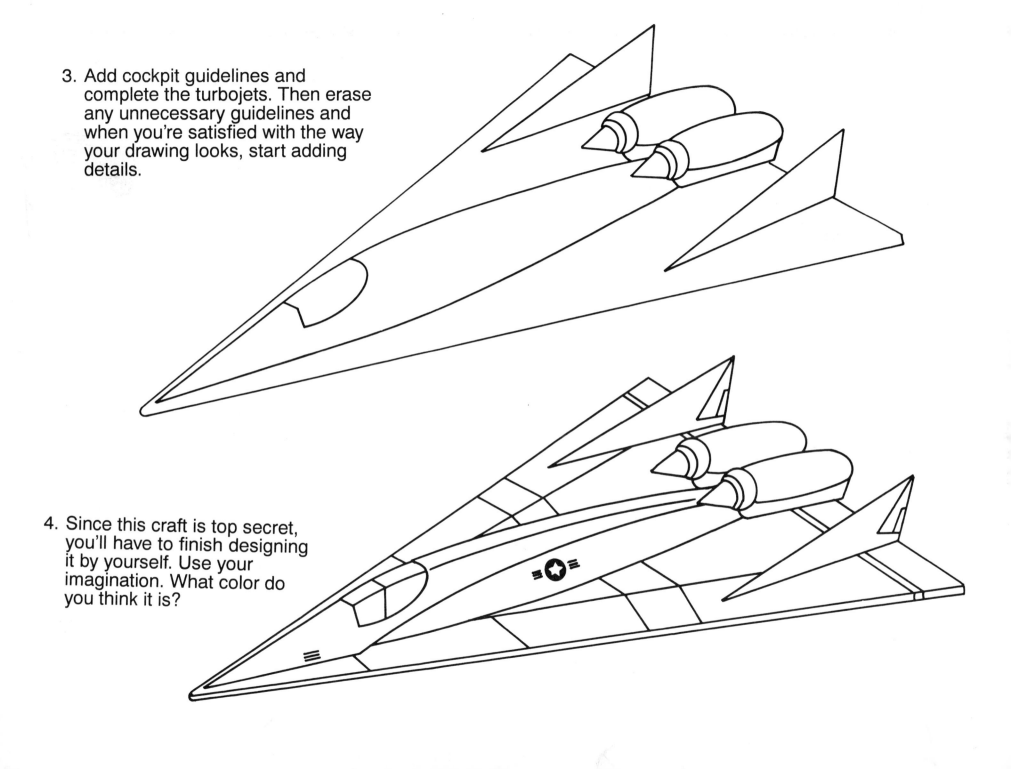

3. Add cockpit guidelines and complete the turbojets. Then erase any unnecessary guidelines and when you're satisfied with the way your drawing looks, start adding details.

4. Since this craft is top secret, you'll have to finish designing it by yourself. Use your imagination. What color do you think it is?

A-10 THUNDERBOLT II (WARTHOG)

The Warthog is like a flying tank. Heavily armored, the low flying, slow
flying 'Hog' has only one mission — close air support of ground troops.

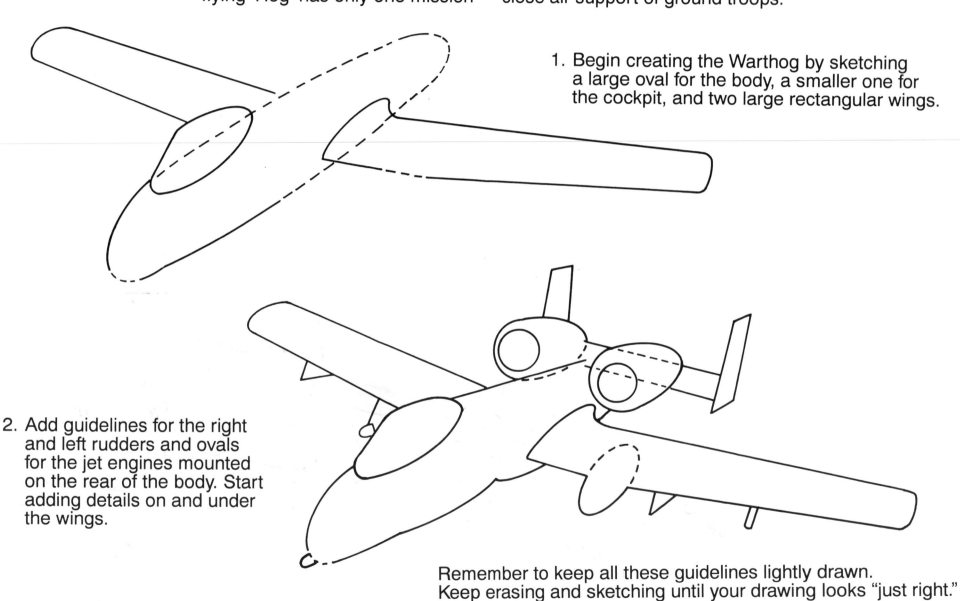

1. Begin creating the Warthog by sketching
   a large oval for the body, a smaller one for
   the cockpit, and two large rectangular wings.

2. Add guidelines for the right
   and left rudders and ovals
   for the jet engines mounted
   on the rear of the body. Start
   adding details on and under
   the wings.

Remember to keep all these guidelines lightly drawn.
Keep erasing and sketching until your drawing looks "just right."

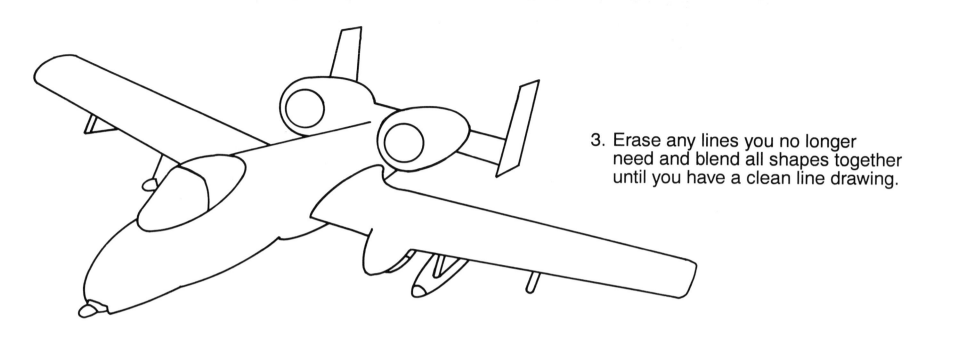

3. Erase any lines you no longer
   need and blend all shapes together
   until you have a clean line drawing.

4. Add details to finish the A-10. Fill in
   the jet engines with black to show
   depth. Add the right and left ailerons.
   They allow the plane to "roll," or in
   combination with the rudders, to
   turn. Finally, add camouflage coloring
   for a dramatic effect.

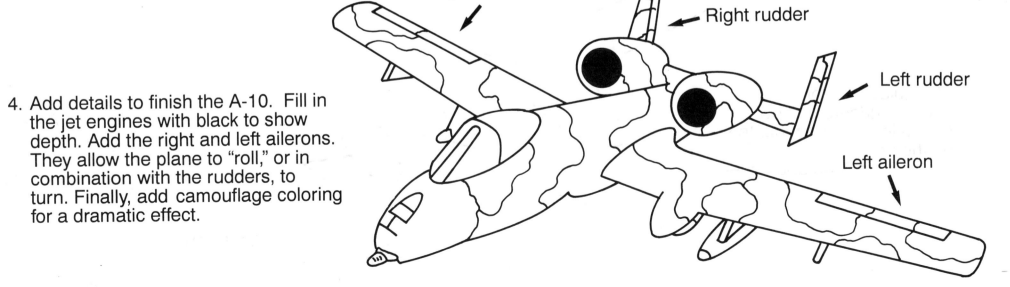

Right aileron

Right rudder

Left rudder

Left aileron

CONSOLIDATED B-24J LIBERATOR

This big and boxy aircraft was a high-altitude, heavy bomber during World War II.

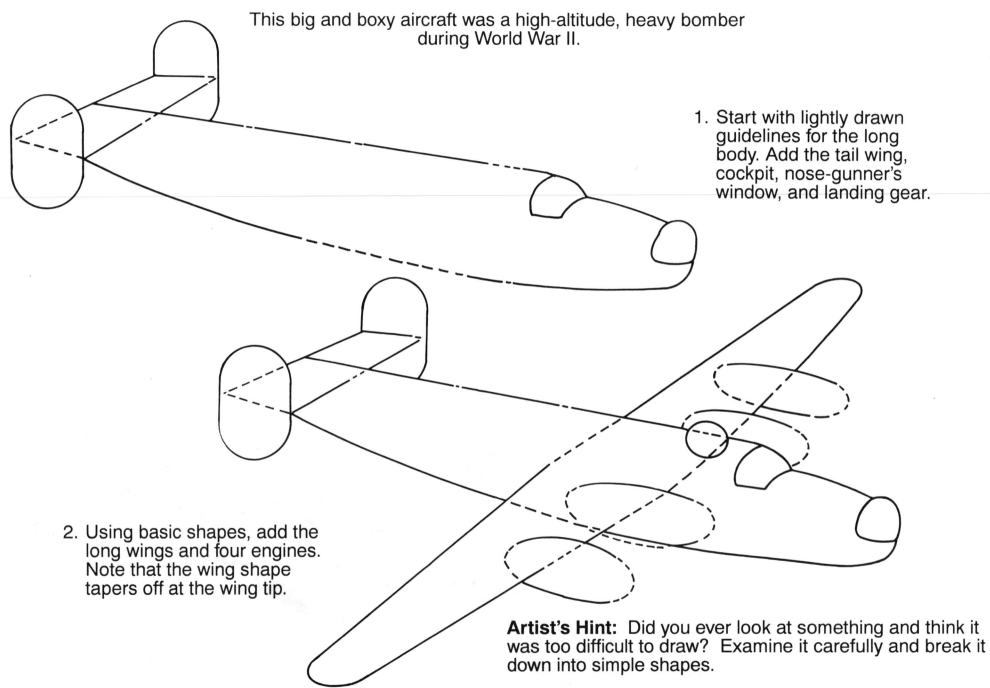

1. Start with lightly drawn guidelines for the long body. Add the tail wing, cockpit, nose-gunner's window, and landing gear.

2. Using basic shapes, add the long wings and four engines. Note that the wing shape tapers off at the wing tip.

Artist's Hint: Did you ever look at something and think it was too difficult to draw? Examine it carefully and break it down into simple shapes.

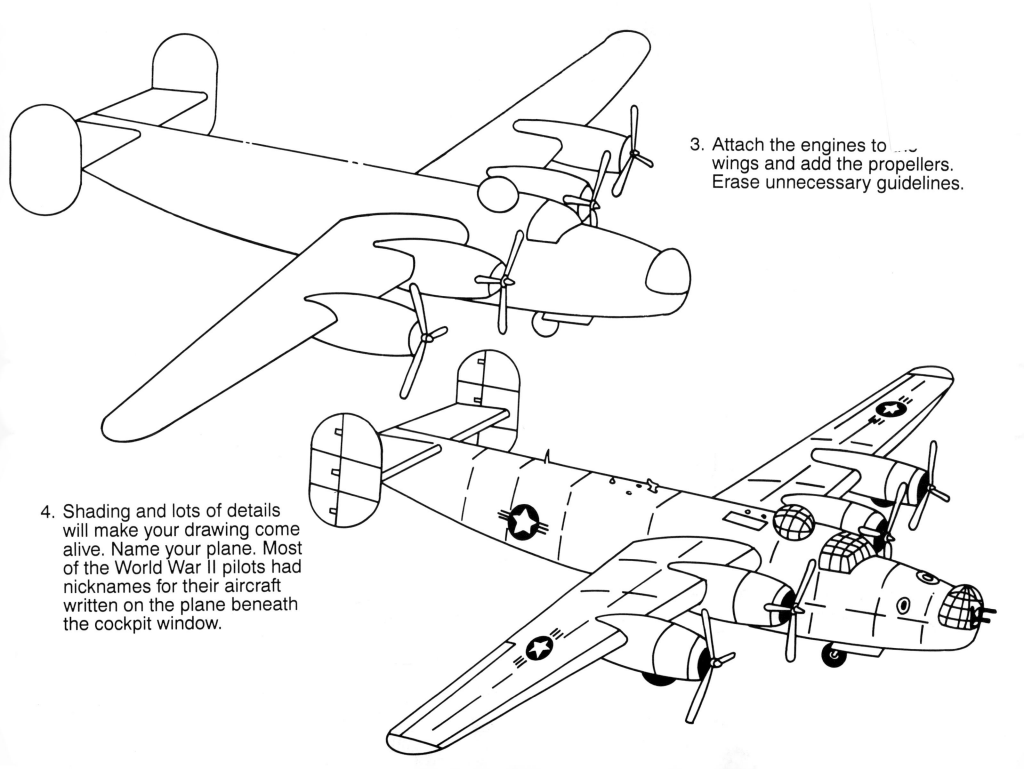

3. Attach the engines to the wings and add the propellers. Erase unnecessary guidelines.

4. Shading and lots of details will make your drawing come alive. Name your plane. Most of the World War II pilots had nicknames for their aircraft written on the plane beneath the cockpit window.

F-16 FIGHTING FALCON

The F-16 can be used as a fighter plane or as a light bomber.

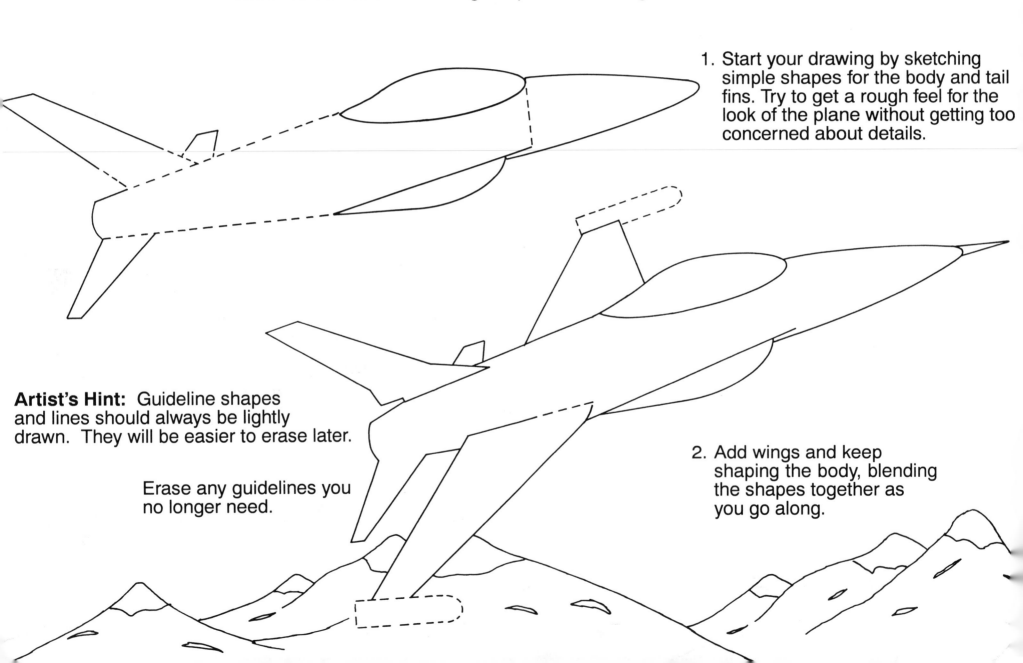

1. Start your drawing by sketching simple shapes for the body and tail fins. Try to get a rough feel for the look of the plane without getting too concerned about details.

Artist's Hint: Guideline shapes and lines should always be lightly drawn. They will be easier to erase later.

Erase any guidelines you no longer need.

2. Add wings and keep shaping the body, blending the shapes together as you go along.

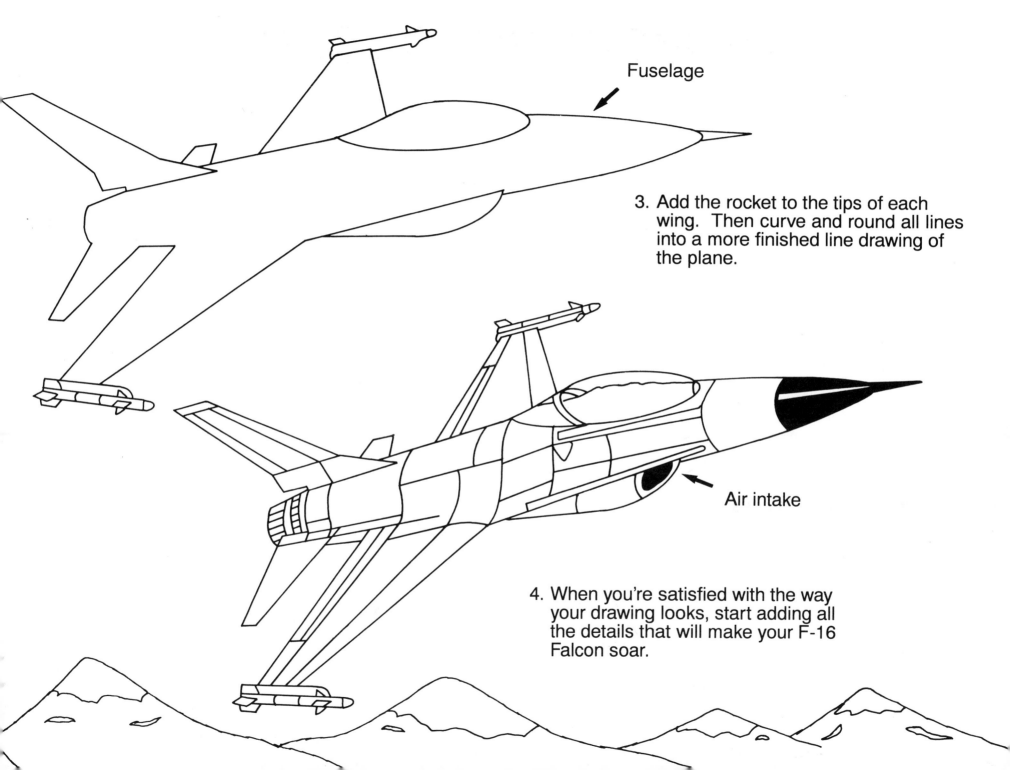

Fuselage

3. Add the rocket to the tips of each wing. Then curve and round all lines into a more finished line drawing of the plane.

Air intake

4. When you're satisfied with the way your drawing looks, start adding all the details that will make your F-16 Falcon soar.

GRUMMAN X-29

The forward wings of this experimental airplane
enable it to be much more agile in flight.

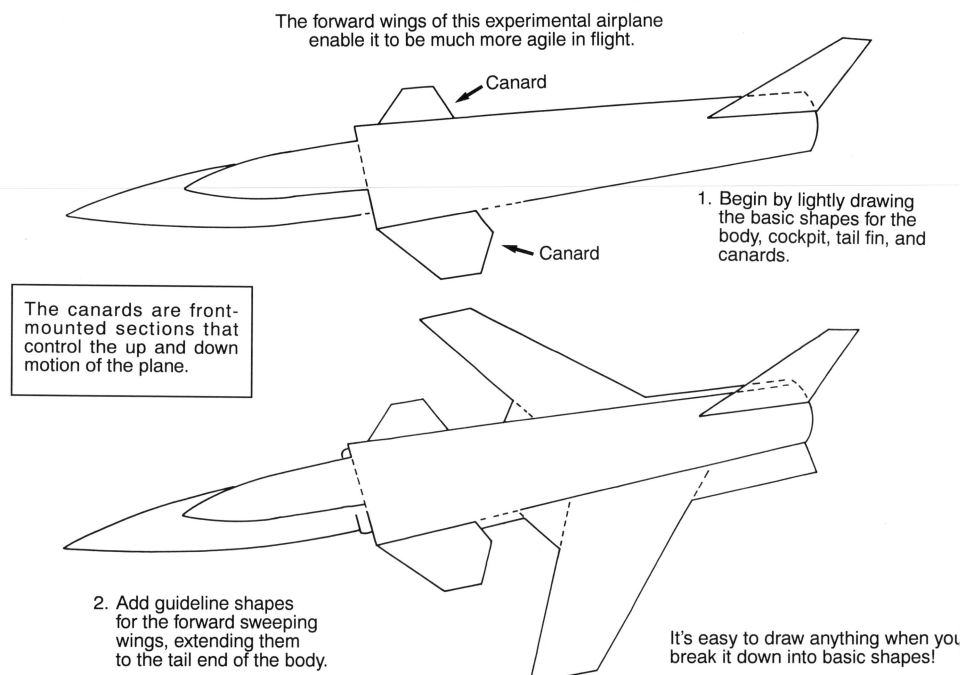

Canard

Canard

1. Begin by lightly drawing
the basic shapes for the
body, cockpit, tail fin, and
canards.

The canards are front-
mounted sections that
control the up and down
motion of the plane.

2. Add guideline shapes
for the forward sweeping
wings, extending them
to the tail end of the body.

It's easy to draw anything when you
break it down into basic shapes!

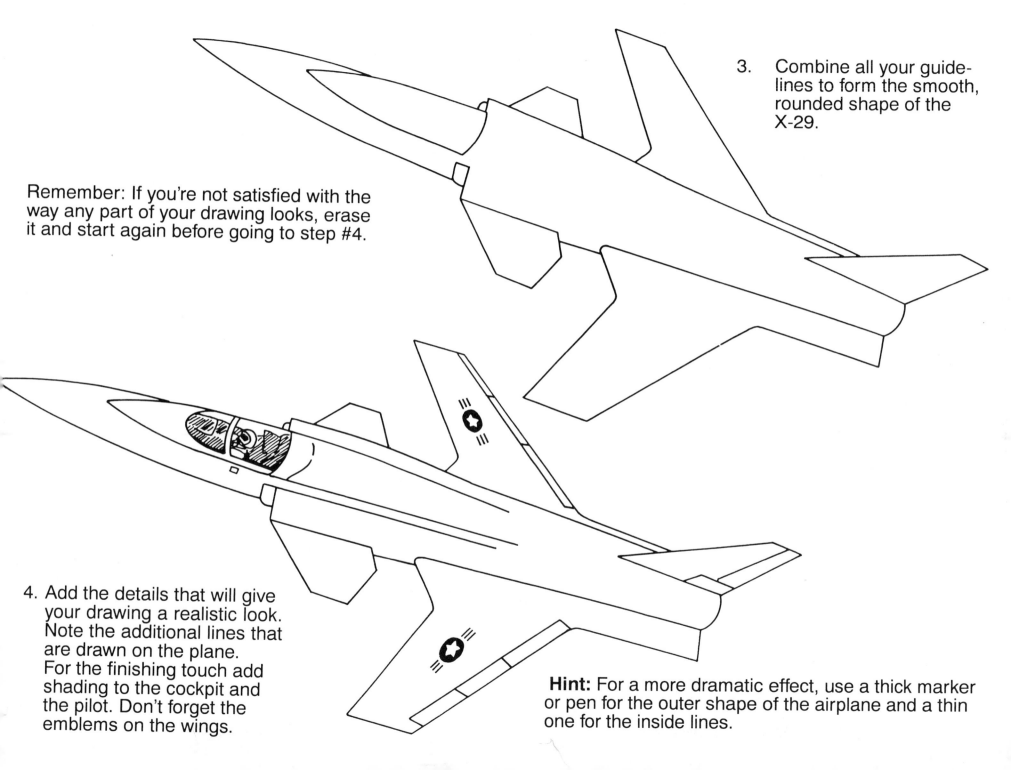

3. Combine all your guide-lines to form the smooth, rounded shape of the X-29.

Remember: If you're not satisfied with the way any part of your drawing looks, erase it and start again before going to step #4.

4. Add the details that will give your drawing a realistic look. Note the additional lines that are drawn on the plane. For the finishing touch add shading to the cockpit and the pilot. Don't forget the emblems on the wings.

Hint: For a more dramatic effect, use a thick marker or pen for the outer shape of the airplane and a thin one for the inside lines.

CESSNA SKYHAWK

The easy-to-fly Skyhawk is one of the most popular private planes in the world.

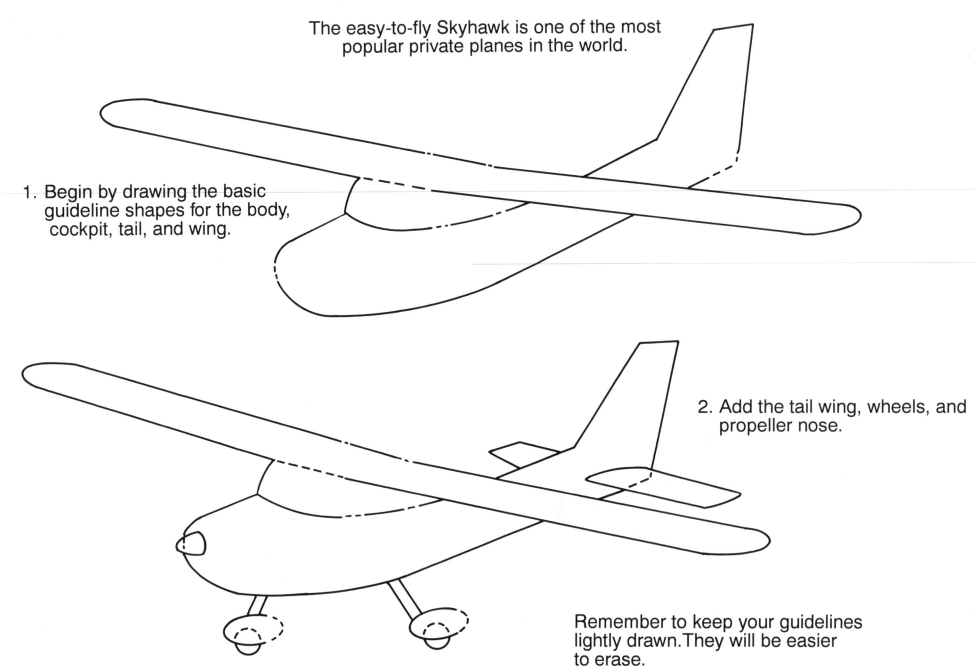

1. Begin by drawing the basic guideline shapes for the body, cockpit, tail, and wing.

2. Add the tail wing, wheels, and propeller nose.

Remember to keep your guidelines lightly drawn. They will be easier to erase.

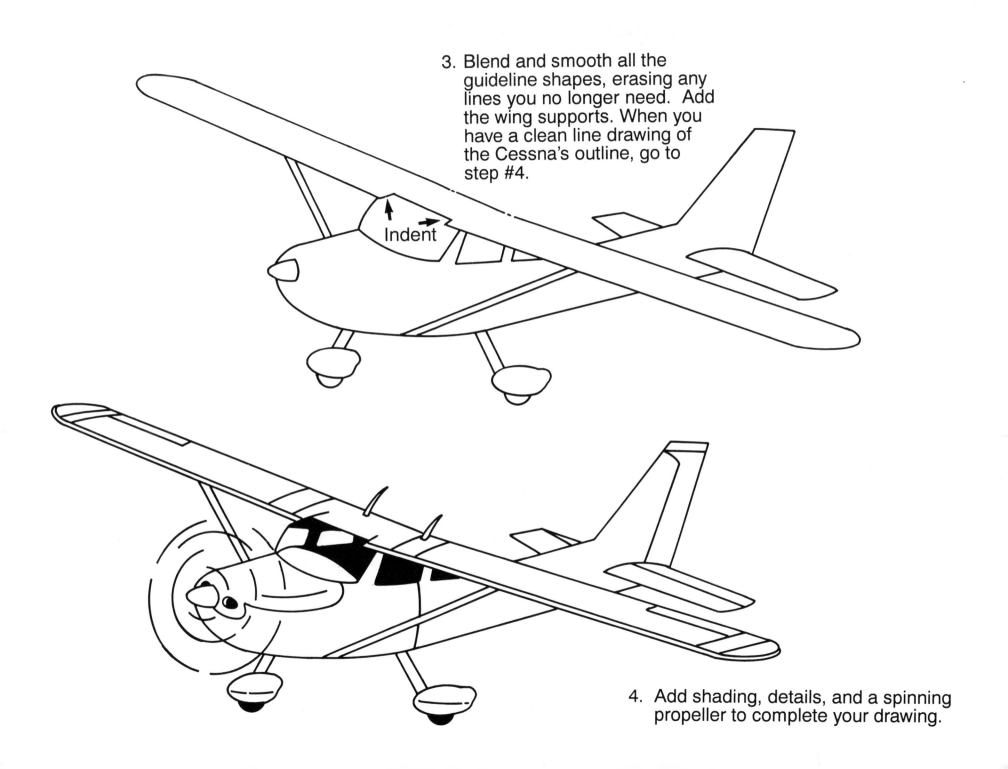

3. Blend and smooth all the guideline shapes, erasing any lines you no longer need. Add the wing supports. When you have a clean line drawing of the Cessna's outline, go to step #4.

Indent

4. Add shading, details, and a spinning propeller to complete your drawing.

MESSERSCHMITT 1106-A

A World War II German airplane fitted
with a primitive radar system.

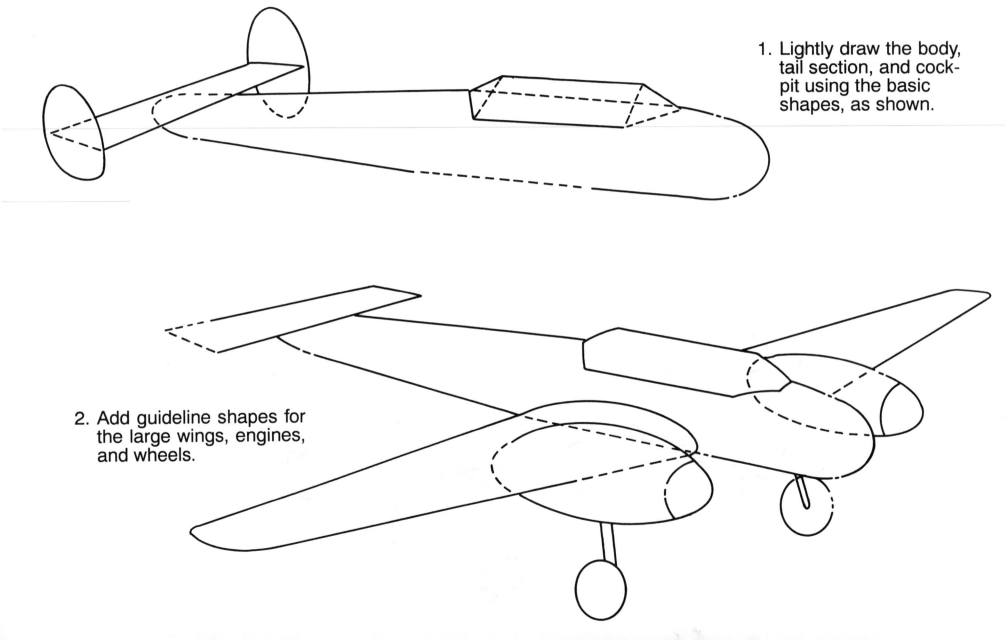

1. Lightly draw the body,
   tail section, and cockpit using the basic
   shapes, as shown.

2. Add guideline shapes for
   the large wings, engines,
   and wheels.

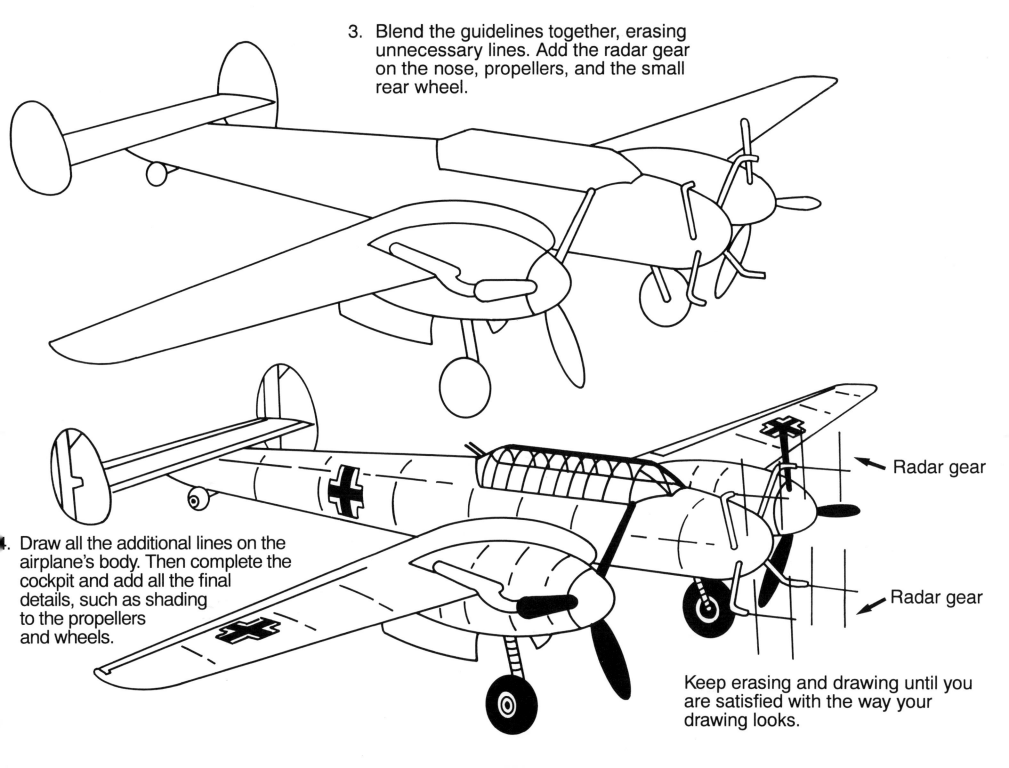

3. Blend the guidelines together, erasing unnecessary lines. Add the radar gear on the nose, propellers, and the small rear wheel.

4. Draw all the additional lines on the airplane's body. Then complete the cockpit and add all the final details, such as shading to the propellers and wheels.

Radar gear

Radar gear

Keep erasing and drawing until you are satisfied with the way your drawing looks.

PIPER ARCHER II

The Piper Archer II is a four-seater, low wing, deluxe private plane.

1. Begin the Piper by first drawing a large oval for the fuselage. Then add the other basic shapes and connecting guide-lines as shown.

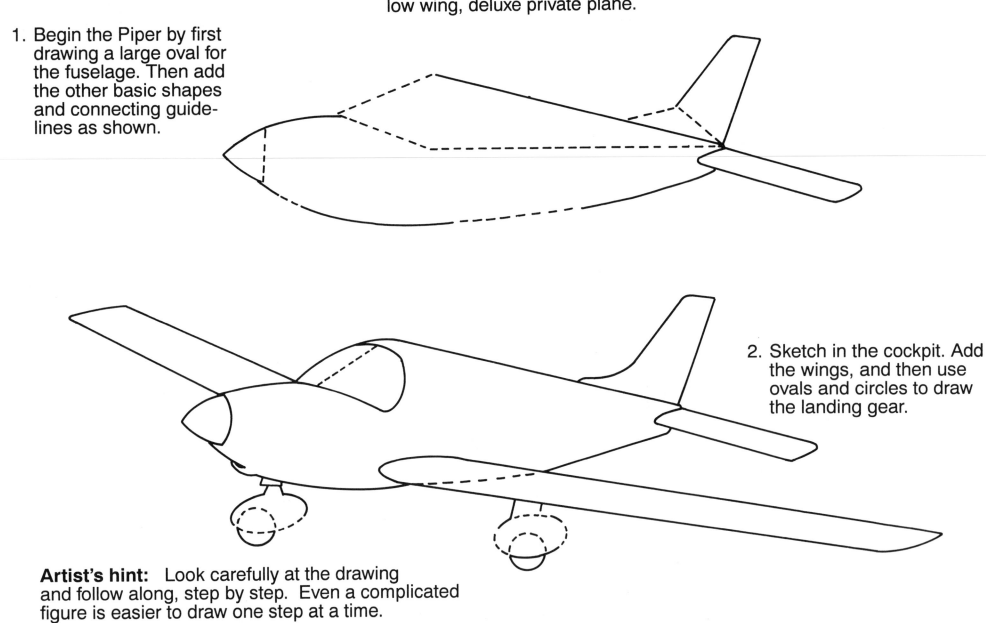

2. Sketch in the cockpit. Add the wings, and then use ovals and circles to draw the landing gear.

Artist's hint: Look carefully at the drawing and follow along, step by step. Even a complicated figure is easier to draw one step at a time.

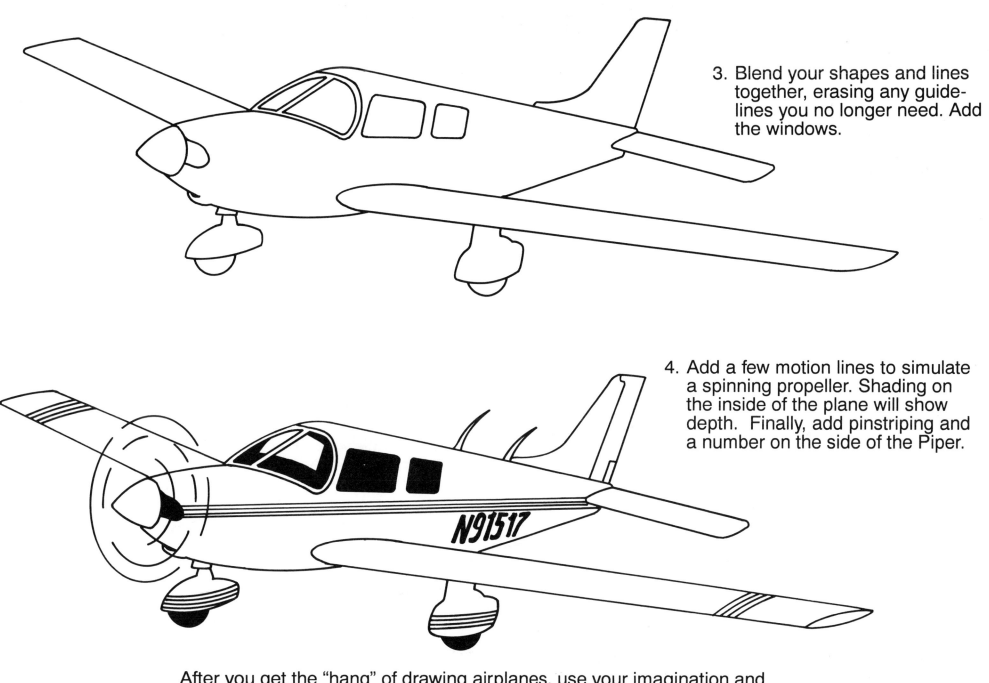

3. Blend your shapes and lines together, erasing any guide-lines you no longer need. Add the windows.

4. Add a few motion lines to simulate a spinning propeller. Shading on the inside of the plane will show depth. Finally, add pinstriping and a number on the side of the Piper.

N91517

After you get the "hang" of drawing airplanes, use your imagination and create a scene with several different planes in it. Then start designing you own flying machines.

V-22 OSPREY

The Osprey takes off like a helicopter
and flies like an airplane.

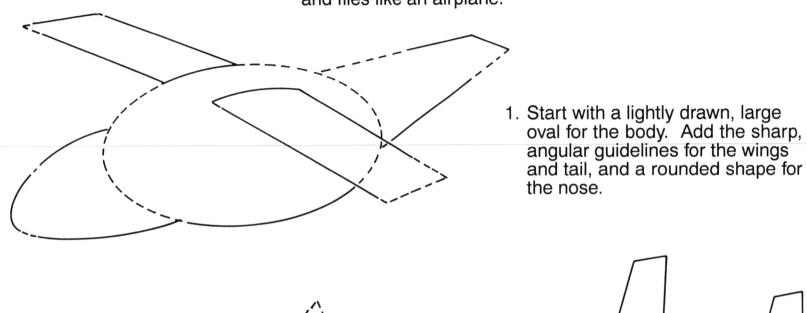

1. Start with a lightly drawn, large
   oval for the body. Add the sharp,
   angular guidelines for the wings
   and tail, and a rounded shape for
   the nose.

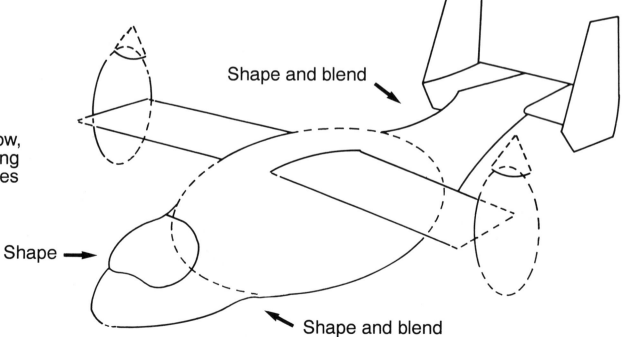

Shape and blend

2. Add the tail fins, cockpit window,
   and the tilting rotors on the wing
   tips. Begin blending the shapes
   as indicated.

Shape →

Shape and blend

3. Combine the shapes into one smooth outline form. Keep erasing and drawing until your lines are just right.

The Osprey's rotors on the end of each wing can be tilted forward. This allows the craft to fly straight up like a helicopter or forward like a conventional airplane.

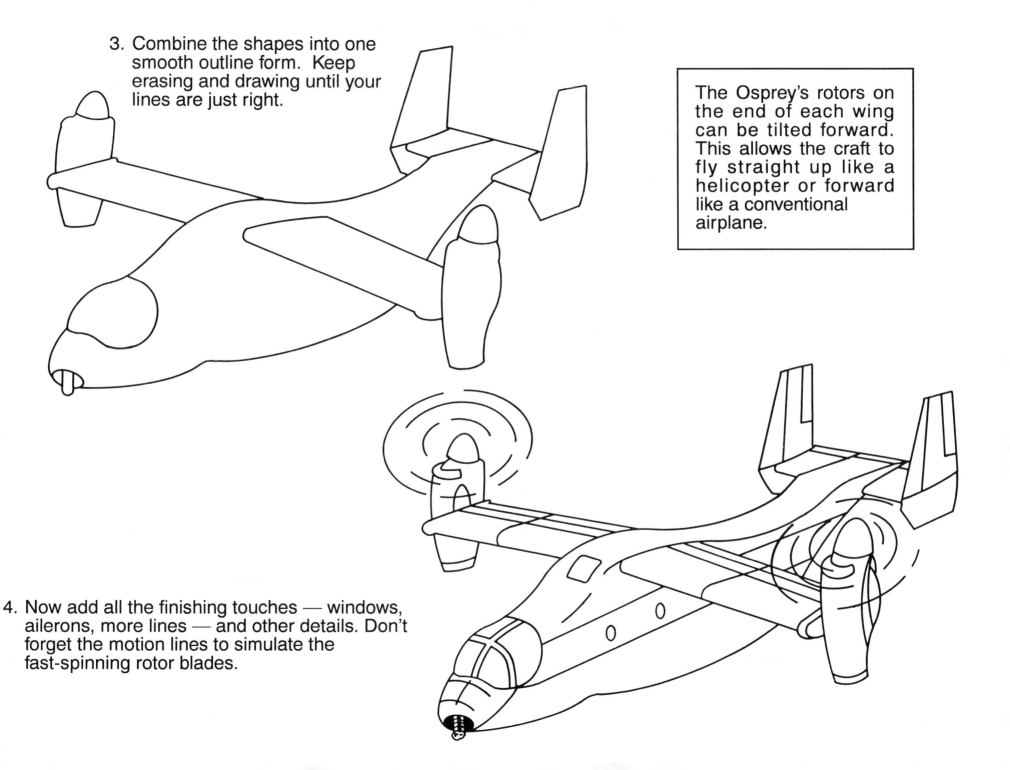

4. Now add all the finishing touches — windows, ailerons, more lines — and other details. Don't forget the motion lines to simulate the fast-spinning rotor blades.

EFA EUROFIGHTER

The Eurofighter is being developed by several European countries.
The front-mounted canards make it a very agile aircraft.

1. Begin your drawing by sketching
   basic shapes for the body, nose,
   cockpit, tail, and canard.

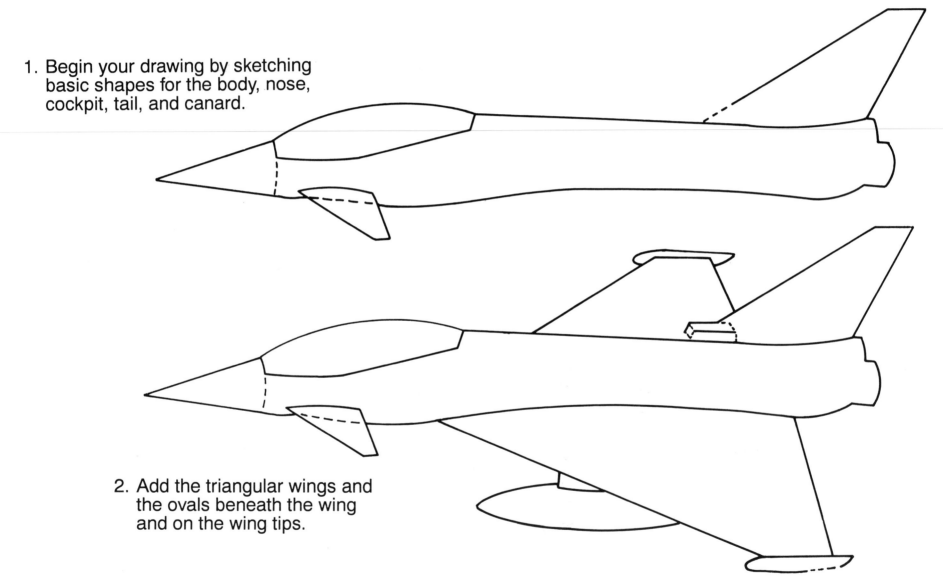

2. Add the triangular wings and
   the ovals beneath the wing
   and on the wing tips.

Remember to keep your guidelines lightly drawn.

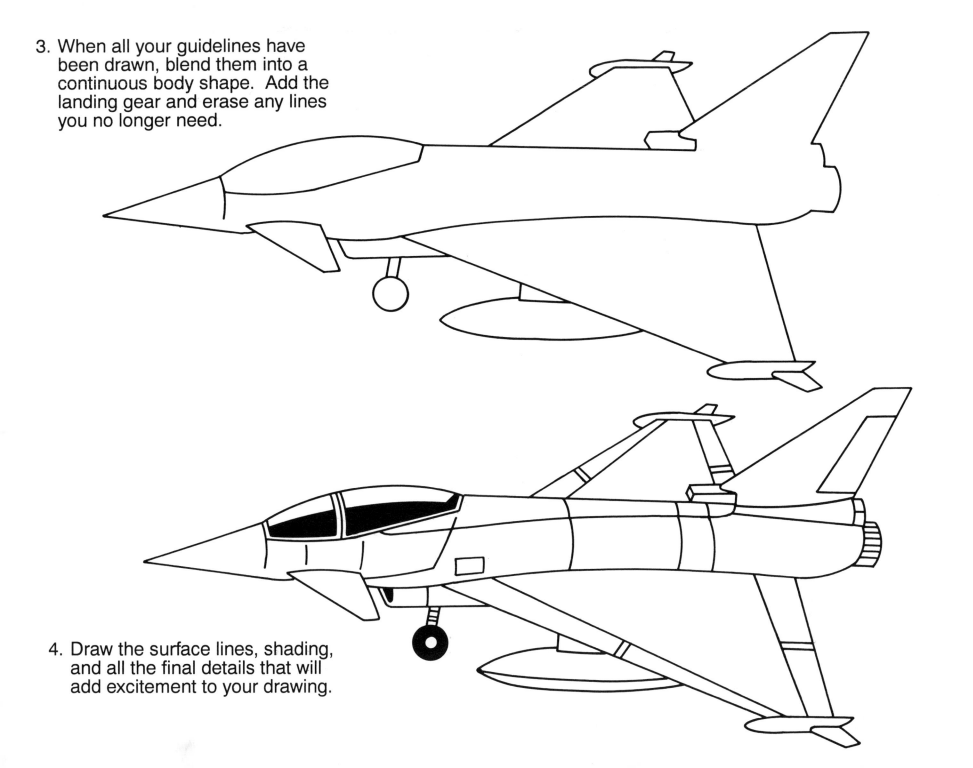

3. When all your guidelines have been drawn, blend them into a continuous body shape. Add the landing gear and erase any lines you no longer need.

4. Draw the surface lines, shading, and all the final details that will add excitement to your drawing.

GRUMMAN E-2C HAWKEYE

This surveillance airplane has an advanced radar system
mounted on top of its fuselage. The Hawkeye is capable of detecting
other airborne craft hundreds of miles away.

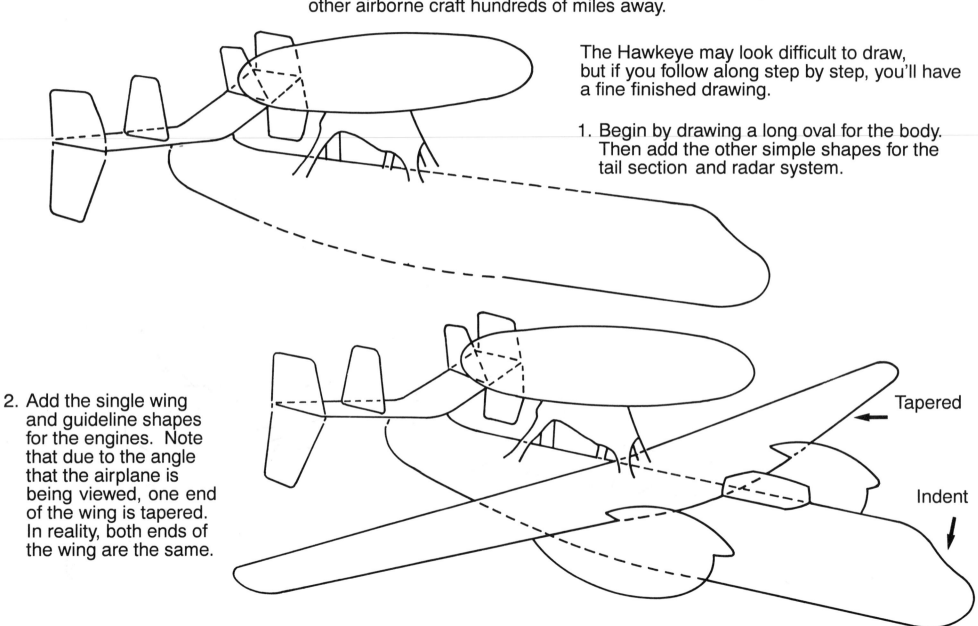

The Hawkeye may look difficult to draw,
but if you follow along step by step, you'll have
a fine finished drawing.

1. Begin by drawing a long oval for the body.
   Then add the other simple shapes for the
   tail section and radar system.

2. Add the single wing
   and guideline shapes
   for the engines. Note
   that due to the angle
   that the airplane is
   being viewed, one end
   of the wing is tapered.
   In reality, both ends of
   the wing are the same.

Tapered

Indent

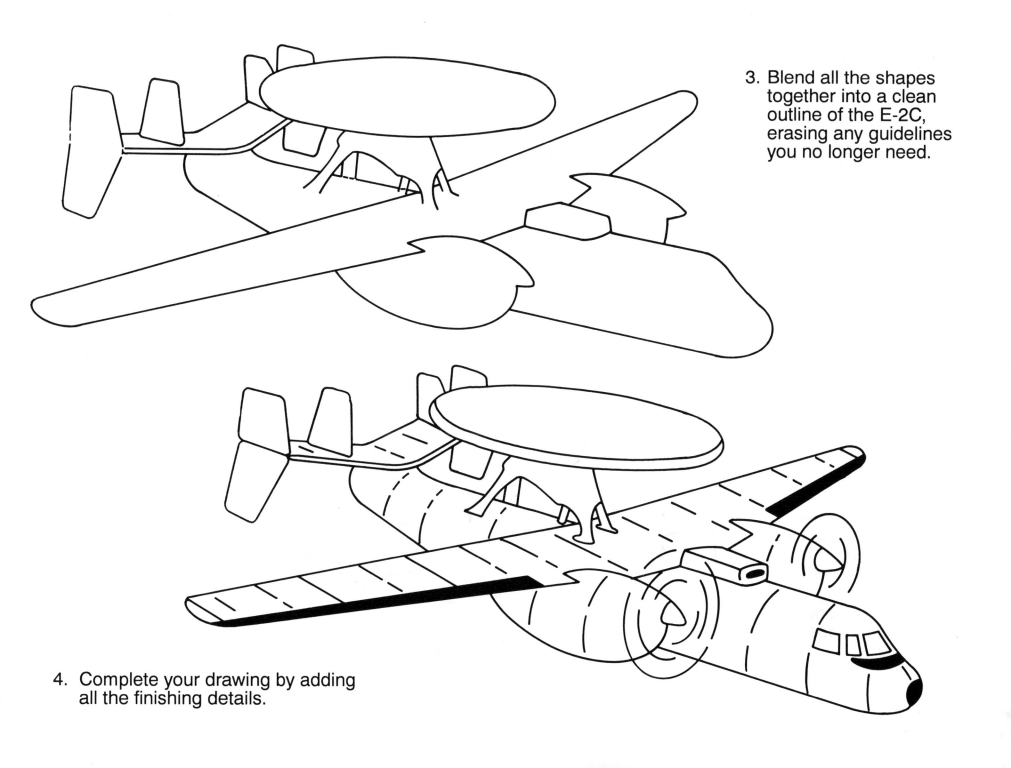

3. Blend all the shapes together into a clean outline of the E-2C, erasing any guidelines you no longer need.

4. Complete your drawing by adding all the finishing details.

LEAR JET 31

This Lear Jet features a high-energy braking system
which enables it to land on very short runways.
It can travel 1,875 miles without refueling.

1. Start by lightly drawing guideline shapes for the body and cockpit.

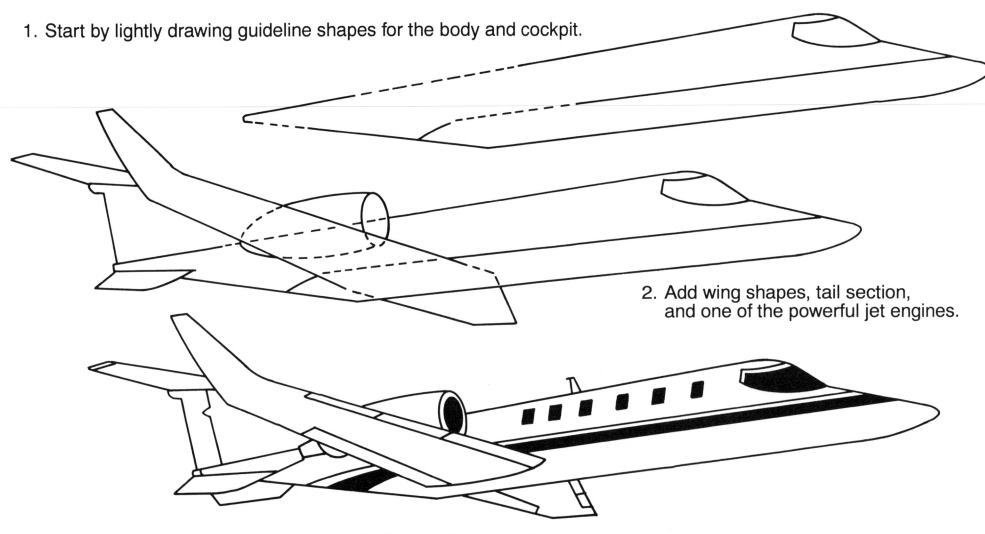

2. Add wing shapes, tail section,
   and one of the powerful jet engines.

3. Blend and round all your shapes and lines into one continuous body,
   erasing as you go along. Finish your Lear Jet by adding windows,
   shading and other details.

Use the following pages to create your own cars, trucks, and things that fly.